THE PROTECTOR

with love

Karina

Praise for the Authors

... reflective glimpse into the life of a strong-willed yet kind-hearted woman ...

—**Prof (Dr) Rajiv Mathur,**
Partner MIGS Global Consulting Pvt Ltd,
Regional Advisor, Asia – OSPAs

... captures the extraordinary life of India's first female bodyguard. An empowering tale ... that inspires us to defy limits and encourages many young women ...

——**Kunwar Vikram Singh**
Chairman CAPSI and Chairman
of Lancers Risk Consulting

... not just a celebrity in the Security Industry but also a TEDx speaker, a beauty queen, a self-defence trainer, a successful entrepreneur, and much more.

——**Lt Bhaskar Shukla**
Ex- Indian Navy, CSO Vatika Group,
CPP, CISM, CSCSS, MHRM

... an outstanding security professional. A beauty with brains ...

—**Sheila Ponnosamy**
Operations Director Mainguard International (S) Pte Ltd,
Board of Governors Indian Institute of Security and Safety Management

Grit, determination, and an unwavering passion ... a true extension of her relentless spirit. A must-read!

—**Monika Pandey**
Marketing Consultant

... a trailblazer who shattered stereotypes to excel in a male-dominated industry ... an inspiration ... an awe-inspiring and compelling narrative of courage, determination, and breaking barriers and a must-read for audiences of all ages.

—**Major Saurabh Srivastava**

THE PROTECTOR

THE EXPLOSIVE TRUE STORY OF
INDIA'S FIRST FEMALE BODYGUARD

VEENA GUPTA
KAMINI KUSUM

An imprint of
Srishti Publishers & Distributors

Srishti Publishers & Distributors
A unit of AJR Publishing LLP
212A, Peacock Lane
Shahpur Jat, New Delhi – 110 049

editorial@srishtipublishers.com

First Published by Bold,
an imprint of Srishti Publishers & Distributors in 2025

10 9 8 7 6 5 4 3 2 1

This is a work of non-fiction based on the author's own experience. While due care has been taken by the authors and publisher to verify contents at press time, certain technical terms, methods and tactics have been omitted/modified for privacy and security reasons. The views expressed are not intended to hurt the sentiments of any individual, community, sect, group, institution or religion. Actual names of people and places have been changed to protect their privacy.

Printed and bound in India.

To all the
women protectors.

—Veena Gupta

To all the women
who dare to break stereotypes.

—Kamini Kusum

Welcome to the World of the Protector

I noticed that two young men on a bike were hounding the car in which the client was travelling. They were riding their bike very erratically and dangerously and zooming very close to the car. I was informed over the walkie-talkie by the CPO sitting in the car that the driver was feeling worried that he would either hit the bike or some other bystander due to their rash driving. He was using all his skills to keep the car on the road, but the two on the bike kept hounding him. I also realized the clients were feeling unsafe and insecure in the car.

The incident of Princess Diana's car crash due to the paparazzi hounding them was fresh in everyone's mind. I realized I had to take control of the situation in a way that did not endanger anyone's life – my client, my team and also the bikers... I instructed the driver to bring our car forward, honking loudly at the bike. The two men who were now focusing on the foreigners inside the car were surprised by the loud honking and they jerked away from the car. We immediately brought our car in between their bike and the other car…

I immediately visualized the road ahead. I knew there was a left turn, which would be a route back to the hotel. I immediately screamed this into the walkie-talkie. He was gripping the handle on the door hard as the car was swerving again and again to avoid hitting the paparazzi or the other car. As we neared the turn, we kept our car stable and exactly parallel to the client's car… The car suddenly took a left. It was now time for the Protector to do her duty. It was time to do or die.

Contents

Prologue

It was the winter of February 2022. I was relaxing in my apartment, sitting by the window with the curtains pulled aside. The rays of the sun shone through the windowpane and caressed my cheeks, bringing a smile to my face. The last few days had been hectic. I had been on my toes, providing EP (executive protection) to a client throughout the period of his stay in India. I had hardly any time to rest before I started packing my bags for Dubai. I had to make logistic arrangements for my Dubai office. This had been on my mind for some time, but the pandemic had thrown a wet blanket on my global aspirations.

I pulled out a stool and stretched out my legs on it. I had been craving for some time for myself, to sit carefree in my apartment in my pyjamas. I closed my eyes, but my mind wandered to the difficult period of the last two years. My EP business had taken a hit. Although I had to shut down my global operations since tourism and travelling had drastically declined, I still managed to survive and profitably run my business. The credit goes to my loyal clients and, of course, my never-say-die attitude, which had been cultivated in me from my childhood. However, the biggest loss I suffered during the pandemic, which was irrevocable, was my father's death.

My thoughts were interrupted by my housekeeper's voice, saying, "Didi, *chai*."

I opened my eyes. She was standing with a tray in her hands and offered me a cup of tea.

"Didi, this is ginger tea. You will feel relaxed. Can I bring anything else for you?" she asked.

"No, that's fine," I replied, sitting up straight and placing the cup on the stool.

I started sipping the tea and my mind wandered back to the years that I had put into the security industry. It has been a journey of almost two decades. People knew me as a female bodyguard. The print and digital media had shone a spotlight on me as India's first female bodyguard. My self-defence workshops were quite popular. The journey had certainly not been an easy one, but that is how I was – a rebel (as some say), who did what she wanted. It is easy to demean or brand a woman as a rebel if she tries to take up a profession that is conventionally considered a male bastion. However, it did not bother me as no one was going to bring food to my table. I am fortunate that I love my work and am passionate about it and, most importantly, earn well from it. My thoughts brought a smile to my face.

Just then, my phone, which was lying on the bed, rang.

I picked it up. The call was from an unknown number.

"Hi, am I speaking to Veena Gupta?" It was a man on the other side.

"Yes, this is Veena here," I replied.

"Veena, this is Prashant calling on behalf of Google India. I am glad to inform you that you have been selected as one of the Google icons in India for this Women's Day."

I was a little sceptical and suspected that it could even be a prank call as I used to get some of those, too.

"Could you please explain the matter in detail?" I asked.

"Google India is running a campaign called 'Bolne se hoga #SearchForChange' to honour women who have been doing inspiring work in different areas. You are doing an amazing job as a self-defence instructor and undoubtedly, your profession – that of a female bodyguard – is so inspiring. There are other empowered women, too, who will be honoured as a part of this campaign. Some celebrities from films and sports are also a part of this campaign. For this, you need to come to Mumbai for a photo shoot. We will use the photos to prepare banners that would be put up across cities with an inspiring caption," he explained.

I listened to him quietly. He named a few women, like a lathi-kathi trainer, an entrepreneur, a shehnai player, a kathak dancer, etc., who had been selected to be honoured on Women's Day.

He added, "We will take care of your travel and stay in Mumbai. Let me know when you would be free to come for the photo shoot. Everything has to be ready well before March 8, i.e., Women's Day."

I already had a packed schedule in the first two weeks of March. So, I told Prashant that I could come to Mumbai in the last week of February. He told me that someone from his team would call again and provide further details.

Though I had been honoured by several organizations, this was extremely gratifying. I was still a little sceptical about it. Was I really being honoured by Google India? Then my heart and mind questioned my scepticism. After all, I had worked so hard all these years and beaten all odds. I had challenged the status quo and made a mark in the security industry. I deserved it.

I was overwhelmed. I thought of calling up Sana, my daughter, and giving her the good news. Then I remembered that she was out of town for her work. I decided to wait until everything was finalized.

A couple of days later, someone called me again with further details. A few emails were exchanged and finally, my flight tickets and accommodation details were sent to me. I travelled to Mumbai on February 26. I was received by someone at the airport and taken to the hotel where my accommodation had been arranged.

The next day, I was taken to a famous studio in Mumbai. This is where the photo shoot had been planned. I met some other women achievers who were also a part of this campaign. By this time, I was quite excited. I was taken to a vanity van to get ready. I was thrilled to see it. I had heard of film stars using vanity vans but had never thought that I, too, would be using one at some point in time and that such respect would be accorded to me.

At the studio, I was told that my hair would be tied in a French braid. I was given a sponsored sports sweatshirt to wear and my hair was styled. They clicked photographs of me in different poses, and finally the photoshoot came to an end. I was provided with a nice lunch and then I was free.

They told me that they would select the best pictures from among those clicked and prepare banners. These banners would be put up in different places across India on March 8 (Women's Day) and they would send me the details of the spots where I could find them. Before I left, they handed me a big gift basket and an envelope. Later on, when I opened the envelope, I found a cheque in my name. I was surprised and honoured.

While on my flight back to Delhi, I was transported back to my days of struggle. Those harsh words that had been directed towards me and which could dampen anyone's morale started echoing in my mind.

"Bodyguard? Do you mean an escort? Like in that Bollywood movie where Rani Mukherjee plays the role of an escort... you do that?"

"She comes home late in the night. A car always drops her home. How can her character be trusted?"

"She travels frequently. She must be having extramarital affairs."

"She is a careless mother who loves money more than she loves her child."

"She is definitely sleeping with her boss or clients. That is why she has made such progress."

"You, a slim and petite woman, are a bodyguard?"

"You need to meet me in the evening over drinks to get this assignment."

"Stay away, lady. This is not your area."

And so on...

I had faced it all, but nothing could ever stop me.

* * *

March 8, 2022

My daughter rang me and said, "Mamma, come to Cyber City. A huge hoarding featuring you has been put up here by Google. I am so proud of you, Ma."

I drove to Cyber City and, as Sana had said, it was a huge banner showing me in a blue sweatshirt, with braided hair and folded arms, oozing confidence. My name was written just beside my photo. It was captioned: *'Koi ladkiyon wali hobby chuno, martial arts kyun seekhna hai?' Bolne se sab hoga* #SearchForChange.

The people standing there stared first at the banner and then at me. Some of them came to me and asked, "Isn't that you in the banner?" Some googled my name and read more about me. They congratulated me for my achievements and even clicked pictures with me. It was such a wonderful feeling!

My friends and acquaintances sent me pictures of the hoardings featuring me from different places. Google India also posted the banner on their social media handle. After this, congratulatory messages started pouring in. I was delighted and beaming with joy and pride.

Today I am a known and respected name in the security industry, but my journey has been full of challenges. It was my humble beginning that made me strong and ingrained 'protection' in my nature.

Chapter 1
Childhood

I strongly feel that the notion that only men can protect others is incorrect. Women are equally capable of protecting themselves, their families and the society. I say this because I am a woman and work as a bodyguard. In the course of my work, I have provided protection for both men and women. The common perception of a bodyguard is that of a bulky man with huge biceps, but the business of providing personal security goes beyond mere physical stature. Aside from physical fitness, the right attitude is of paramount importance. I was *befikr and bekhauf*! People called me a rebel, and it was a fitting description.

I was born on August 24, 1970, in Tilak Nagar, Delhi and was the third among six siblings. To be honest, I was an unwanted girl child and my birth was not cause for any joy in the family. After two daughters, everybody was hoping for a son to be born. In our society, especially during those days, a family was considered incomplete without a son. And three daughters, one after the other, in a middle-class family, meant that the mother had to keep trying to conceive a son. My grandmother was extremely annoyed at my birth and my mother had to bear the brunt of her angst. She was so displeased that she maintained a distance from my mother. Perhaps that could be the reason I was neglected as a child.

Almost two years later, my younger sister, Rajji, was born, but people say that she brought good luck as after her, my mother gave birth to two sons, Bholu and Chotu, each after a gap of a couple of years. My elder sisters, Dimple and Geetu, were quite beautiful and pampered. Dimple was doing most of the household chores. Since I received the least attention, I started taking up responsibilities on my own. I even did chores that were usually done by boys. I wanted to prove that I was not a daughter, but a son to my parents. I wanted to prove that I was worthy and deserved the same attention that my other siblings received.

I was a tomboy and protective by nature since childhood. I could not tolerate the roadside Romeos who loitered in our lane and stared at my elder sisters when they stepped out of our home. I would place my hands on my waist, look at them coldly and ask belligerently, "Have you never seen girls? Be off with you and mind your own business."

The boys would be shocked, as they did not expect a girl to confront them in this way. Sometimes, I would use other tricks to get rid of them. Sitting at the window, the moment I'd see those eve-teasers walking by our house, I would start singing in a shrill voice, "*Mota pet sadak par let, gadi ayi phat gaya pet*!"

I would sing non-stop in a loud voice till they'd be irritated and acutely embarrassed. Sometimes, they would come to our house and complain to my mother. Then I would jump into the conversation and say sternly, "Stop staring at my sisters and I will stop singing. Anyway, I am just singing a song while sitting inside my home."

My retort was enough to silence them and prove their guilt.

***

My father was a technician who worked in the Army workshop as a store manager. He was a civilian in the Army. I still remember that he would go to the workshop on his bicycle. As children, all of us would eagerly wait for him to bring us something to eat upon his return in the evening. Usually, he brought *pedas* and *jalebis* for us from the canteen. I would wait for my siblings to take their share and then take the packet of jalebis in the end, as it contained the sugar syrup that I relished.

During those days, Murphy's radios were very popular and my father, too, wanted to buy one. He had been saving money for it, but my mother had different plans. Though my mother was not very educated, she was quite foresighted and judicious when it came to financial matters. We had been living on rent in Tilak Nagar and in view of our large family, she was keen to buy a plot of land so that a house with ample rooms could be built.

She suggested as such to my father, saying, "Buying a plot is more important than getting a radio or anything else. We need to save money as our family is big and we have daughters. It is time we think of buying our own house."

She was right. How long could we live in a rented house? My grandparents lived nearby, but since my mother had given birth to so many girls, there was no love left between her and my grandmother. Things had changed between my grandmother and mother, especially after my birth.

So, finally, when my parents had saved enough money, they bought two plots of land in the *kachchi* colony of Nawada. Nestled in Western Delhi, Nawada was a village back then, though it has now changed a lot and also has a metro station. Our house that was built on the plot was designed in the same fashion as those built in villages and small towns. We had rooms, along with a hall that opened out to a concrete veranda which was attached to the kitchen. As we walked down the steps from the veranda, there was some open space until our boundary wall. There was a borewell in one corner, and in the other was our toilet.

We had a couple of rooms on the rooftop as well. During the summers, we would all sleep together on the roof under the open skies. We would sprinkle water on the roof to cool it down and then we would spread our mattresses. This was one of the best parts of having a big family. It was great fun to lie down together and look up at the twinkling stars. We would talk, gossip and laugh together till we'd fall asleep. When I look back, they were happy and carefree days, spent in the company of loved ones.

* * *

I was a naughty child. I could never sit still. With no end to my curiosity, I would try my hands at almost everything. I kept everyone around me on their toes with my mischief. I was four years old when it was decided that I should be sent to school. One fine day, I was taken to an all-girls government school for admission. It was a Hindi medium school, and I was terribly excited as I entered the premises. Even though younger in age than most of my classmates, I never faced any difficulty in my studies. I coped easily with the curriculum as I was an active and intelligent child, according to the teachers.

My parents were happy with me attending school regularly, as I would be busy for at least half the day. My mother had her hands full with my younger sister to take care of, and all she wanted was for the elder kids to keep busy among themselves.

When we were not in school, we spent most part of the day commuting. The school was rather far away and there was no means of transport to get there. My sisters and I had to walk for nearly half an hour to reach the school. As I had my sisters to accompany me, it was a joyful journey. We'd chat and laugh all the way. It would have been boring if I had to walk all by myself. Our school days were filled with pleasant memories. Even though we were girls, our family understood the importance of education and knew the only way for a bright future was through good education.

Since ours was a kachchi colony and not properly developed as yet, fetching drinking water was a tedious task. Even though we had our borewell, we couldn't use that water for drinking. The water, being salty, wasn't even fit for bathing. To fetch the supply of water, which we called *meetha paani,* we had to walk for almost fifteen minutes carrying our buckets and *matkas*. Usually, there was one *tooti* (that is what we called the supply water point) in one colony, and ours was almost at the end of the colony. I took this task of getting water upon myself. The naughty me carried out this task happily. It was a fun chore. To make sure that I was one of the early birds, I would usually get up at four in the morning and line up all our buckets and matkas at the water supply point.

It was usually buzzing with activity. The women would inevitably start having arguments while they waited for the water. It was a common sight in the colony. Shyama aunty from our neighbourhood would, more often than not, be the first one to grumble at the sight of the queue of my buckets. I would only annoy her further by giving her a smug smile. And if she ever said something directly to me, I would give a retort, "Why don't you come earlier to fetch water?"

I would pick up the two *matkas* and one bucket, all full of water to the brim, at the same time. I'd place one matka carefully on my head, and the other on my waist. The bucket remained in my other hand. I would walk home carefully, balancing all three perfectly well. It was quite a feat now when I think of it. I would have a victorious smile on my face when I finally put the matkas and the bucket full of water safely in the kitchen. I was always happy with a job well done, no matter how trivial. This is how I was; trying to find perfection in every little thing I did.

Even today, when my clients send me appreciation emails for the protection services I provide them, they applaud the extra effort I put in to make each and every part of my assignment flawless. I always try to give my hundred per cent to whatever I do. Nobody is perfect, but at least striving for it can lead to wonderful results.

When it came to studies, though I wasn't a rank holder, I had a sharp mind and I would gather things quickly. I was a quick learner and could easily adapt to any situation. When I'd return home from school, I would spend the afternoon diligently with my books. We had a big guava tree in our courtyard, with its branches spreading out over the boundary wall. This guava tree was my favourite place as a child. I would climb up the tree with my books and sit on its thick branches or on the boundary wall where the branches rested. It was a perfect nook as I relished the sweet fruit while revising my lessons. When not doing either, I would keenly gaze at all the passersby below on the street. Being a keen observer, I would keep tabs on the goings on in our neighbourhood and was usually up to date with the latest news.

Another major problem we faced during my growing-up years was the erratic electricity supply. Without kerosene lamps as a backup, it would have been difficult to carry on. At night, when often there would be power cuts, we siblings would gather around the lanterns and study. I had a favourite spot in the house as well. While my siblings studied sitting on the floor, I would climb the stairs that led to the rooftop. I would sit mid-way on the stairs and study peacefully in my own little corner.

My sisters would say exasperated, "Veenu, why do you have to do something weird always?"

I would just laugh, "I am like this only."

And that was true. I always veered towards things that were out of the ordinary.

At night, after my mother extinguished the lanterns, I would go up to the roof and study under the streetlight, which was close to our house's wall. It wasn't easy, but we always found a way to keep our spirits going strong. We overcame the hurdles with resilience. As I look back at those days of struggle, I realize how they contributed to my character and helped me realize my true potential. Had it not been for the hardships, people wouldn't have known me for what I am today.

* * *

My urge to try out new things, especially those considered unusual for girls, always gave me a kick. I remember an amusing incident.

Close to my home, there lived some rickshaw pullers who parked their rickshaws in the parking lot close to their homes. I keenly observed their day to day life from the guava tree; watched them pulling the rickshaws, getting back to their homes to rest after a long tiring day, preparing thick chapattis and then having them with onion and pickle. I found all these observations very interesting.

One evening, I was sitting with my girls' gang, which mainly consisted of the school friends who lived nearby.

I asked them, "Do you want a ride on a rickshaw?"

The girls were curious. They knew my mind could give birth to all sorts of absurd ideas, but they always trusted my initiatives, as they would always turn out to be a lot of fun. So, I, along with my friends, befriended the rickshaw pullers. We sat and chatted with them, and cooked and ate chapattis with them too. Then I started trying out riding the rickshaw, and very soon I was able to ride one quite well.

A girl who can handle rowdies and never hesitates to try out tough things can surely pull a rickshaw too, I thought with a smile on my face. I would take my friends out for a rickshaw rides very often. They would shout and giggle with excitement, much to the amusement of the passersby. Weary of my antics, my mother would cry out in exasperation, "God only knows what else this girl will try her hands at!" And I would laugh in reply.

Along with hardships, my childhood had a plethora of beautiful memories. One of them is the Ram Leela. It was our favourite annual festival. How can I forget the excitement with which I waited for it so eagerly? We were the ones who organized it in our village and I, of course, was an active participant. Usually, girls would take on the role of a feminine character, but the role of Ravan was exclusively reserved for me. Somehow the character of Ravan, with his ten enormous heads, his overpowering body and his roaring voice with attitude, always attracted me. I was in awe of his strength and power.

My friends, always surprised by my preference, would say, "Your choice of character is . . . ." And they wouldn't complete the sentence. I understood what they meant. I was used to such remarks and, to be honest, I rather liked them. Things that were awkward for others tempted me like a flame does to a moth. This taste and temperament for the unusual became part of my inherent nature as I grew up.

* * *

With the good memories were also the bad. Quite often, we hear of child abuse these days. Kids are taught about 'good touch' and 'bad touch' in schools. They are encouraged to speak up and to share any experience. They are made aware of the dangers that they might face. But during our times, there was absolutely no awareness of such abuse. Firstly, a child could hardly understand even when he or she was being abused. And even if he or she did, they stayed tight-lipped and never shared the traumatic experience. The oppressors understood this well, and this gave them to confidence to perpetrate the crime without any fear.

I, too, was touched inappropriately by a rogue when I was a child, and I barely understood that I was being abused. The memory of that incident fills me with anger, especially at my helplessness as a victim. There was an ice-cream seller who came regularly to our colony. He would barter scraps for ice-cream. I, being an outgoing and extroverted child who enjoyed doing things on my own, would stealthily sell the scraps in our house for ice-cream. My siblings would quietly keep a lookout so that our mother didn't get to know. They eagerly waited for their share while I went to the ice-cream seller with the scrap. The hawker would wait for me in front of our house, as he knew I'd always have some scrap material to give him. He would hold me and make me sit in the front seat of his cycle. While doing so, he would touch me inappropriately. I couldn't understand back then why his hands ran over different parts of my body without any reason. I was young and innocent and the only thing on my mind was getting the ice-cream for myself and my siblings.

Yet, I vaguely remember his weird smile when I walked back to my house taking the ice-creams with me. Now I understand how lecherous that smile was. How evil the man was! I wish someone had educated me about good and bad touch back then. I would have been spared the horror and maybe could have got him punished. But that was how the society was back then. Some things were not spoken about and were to be borne in silence.

There are other incidents from my childhood which make me laugh whenever I think of them. They remind me of how innocent I was back then. I was thirteen and barely understood anything related to sex, unlike today's kids, who know much more at a young age. Talking about sex, contraception and condoms was a big taboo then. They were not topics to be spoken about. While playing in the street, I came across a white balloon. It looked dirty, but I was tempted to pick it up. I had always played with colourful balloons, but never a white one. I picked it up and took it home. I washed it properly inside and out and brought it into our hall where Ma was.

The moment my mother saw the white balloon I was about to blow, she shouted, "Throw that away right now! Now!"

"But why?" I looked at her, rather shocked at her outburst.

"Don't ask me any questions. Just throw it away and go and wash your hands," she said, disgust apparent on her face.

I had an inquisitive and logical bent of mind since childhood. I always liked to get to the bottom of things, and wouldn't give up anything without a proper reason to do so. When I continued arguing with my mother, she picked up the spade lying in the corner and hit me with the wooden handle. I was shocked. What was so mysterious about the balloon that it had irked my mother so much? It only made me more curious. But before I finally threw it away, I was given a good thrashing with the spade.

When I look back, I realize what a fool I was. But it was neither my fault nor my mother's. If talking about such important matters as sex and contraception was such a taboo, such ignorance was bound to prevail. My mother couldn't even tell me what it was. Thankfully, our society has changed a lot since then. Though the importance of sex education is gaining ground, there is a lot to be done. I still feel we need to openly talk about it.

* * *

My inclination towards athletics was natural. I was a tomboy who spent most of my time outdoors. I would be found running, jumping and playing as soon as I was back from school and was done with my chores. How could I keep myself away from the sports competitions that were held at my school then? My school paid special attention towards the development of sports and even sent students to participate in bigger tournaments. I participated in most of the athletic events. Shot-put was my favourite sport, though I took part in running and kabaddi too. I was lean but strong and had an athletic body. I was a natural and soon started winning prizes in various sports at my school.

The school authorities took notice, and I was sent out for district and zonal-level competitions. I was quite happy as I got a chance to travel. I truly enjoyed all the appreciation I received. I even participated in state-level tournaments in various sports. It was a great learning experience. Later I learnt gymnastics as well when I was in my senior secondary school, thanks to my athletic build and flexible body.

In spite of the success I achieved, I knew I wouldn't be able to make a career out of sports. I did not have the kind of support that was required. My parents had hardly anything to say about my professional career. They had enough on their plate. They went with the flow, trying hard to provide for the family. My mother was always busy with the household chores and taking care of my younger brothers. My father did try to keep up with our work when he was free, and from time to time, checked our progress in our studies.

After completing my matriculation, I enrolled in a senior secondary school in Uttam Nagar. I was an average-looking, lean and thin girl, but I could see the development my body was going through. All the girls in my school wore bras, but I was still wearing a chemise. When the girls talked about cup sizes, I would keenly listen to them. I wondered why I was still pulling on without one. Why didn't my mother ever tell me to wear a bra? Even my elder sisters wore bras.

After reaching home one day, I closed the door and stood in front of the mirror. I kept gazing at myself for a while. My body was changing with the onset of puberty. I had a smile on my lips as I imagined myself wearing a bra and how it would change my appearance. I wondered what cup size would fit me best. I decided I would talk to my mother and buy one for myself.

When I told my mother that all my friends wore bras and that I too wanted one, she gave me a curt reply: "You don't need one."

And yet again the logical girl in me argued, "But why not, Ma?"

"Don't look at what the other girls are doing. Don't compare yourself to others. I told you, you don't need one. Just wear two chemises and that's fine for you."

Wearing two chemises! I found that bit of advice weird, but saw no point in arguing with my mother. I could never understand why I wasn't allowed to wear a bra till I had almost reached my last year in school. She might have had her reasons. My elder sisters were beautiful but had had bad experiences with eve-teasers. So, would wearing a bra make me look attractive and invite harassment? Or was it just because my mother lacked the same attachment to me as she did to my other siblings? My mind was searching for a valid reason, but I couldn't arrive at one.

I saw my friends getting their eyebrows and upper lips done. They looked neat and pretty after. I had a little growth of hair on my upper lip. My friends soon started calling me '*muchchhad*'. Though they were exaggerating, I was annoyed. I tried to shut them up but realized that I would really look better if it was cleaned. I went to my mother and requested her to allow me to get my eyebrows and upper lip done.

And yet again, her reply was a 'no'.

I pleaded, "Ma, please, I look like a boy. At least, let me get my upper lip done."

"Don't worry about what others say. You are fine the way you are."

That was her reply, and my request was dismissed. And I couldn't do anything.

At times, I seriously doubted if my mother deliberately wanted me to remain unfeminine. It was difficult to gauge what she did. Was it for my benefit? At most times, it didn't seem to be. However, I was an obedient child, and I always did what my mother said, willingly or unwillingly. Resting everything aside, today my mother is a strong anchor in my life. Had it not been for her unwavering support at my low points in life, I wouldn't have made it this far.

My father was a disciplined man. He preferred doing most of the domestic stuff which required the services of a plumber, carpenter or an electrician on his own. I, being a curious kid, ever-ready to learn myriad things, would assist my father. I helped him paint the doors, fix the nuts and bolts of the hand pump, and do any cement work needed in the house and, in fact, anything that wasn't usually considered a girl's job. I was a quick learner and was strong. Slowly, I was becoming my father's favourite. I was turning out to be his son.

* * * *

During the month of Sawan, swings were put up in our village at specific places. The womenfolk would gather and sing songs while sitting on the swings. And when ladies gather in one place, gossip is sure to flow. I, along with my friends, would also go there to play and enjoy ourselves. That is where I got to know that bandits had been frequenting villages, including ours. I learnt that they not only took away goods but also picked up beautiful young girls. The ladies talked about what happened to those girls and what the bandits did with them. All I could conclude was that something bad happened to those girls.

My mother was especially concerned, as there were four girls in our house. And then one unfortunate day, the bandits eyed our house. During that eerie silence of the night when all of us were sleeping, my father woke up hearing footsteps close to the veranda. He realized that the bandits had reached our doorstep.

He roared in anger, "Veenu, bring the gun! Let's wake up all the villagers and teach these bandits a lesson!" His loud voice startled all of us and surely the bandits outside as well.

Being associated with the army, he had a fearless attitude. Everyone in our locality knew that our house belonged to Gupta ji, the man from the army. And that he had his own army at home as well. We eight (six siblings and our parents) were no less than an army for outsiders, even though I was the only super-active one among all of my siblings, who would jump to solve any problematic situation without as much as a second thought.

I was sleeping beside the window. Upon hearing my father's voice, I immediately sat up. My father would always call me first for anything. And that day too, when it came to facing the bandits, he took my name.

Grasping the situation, I shouted, "Here, Papa, take the gun. Wake everybody up!" I shouted back.

And then through the slit of the window, we could see the light of a matchstick outside. The bandits had lit a matchstick and climbed on the roof. We waited for a while. Everything was still, and we heard no movement outside. The bandits had left. Later in the morning, we could see their footprints in our *aangan*. That incident infuses a sort of thrill in me even today. What a close encounter with bandits. I surely had a very exciting childhood.

* * *

After finishing my schooling, I enrolled myself in Delhi University for my graduation. Going to college on my own and handling new situations made me smarter and more confident. My independence helped to develop my character. Slowly I was turning from an average-looking girl to an attractive woman, though I was still in my teens.

For the last few years, I had been dreaming of getting into the police or CRPF. I idolized Kiran Bedi, reading everything about her. I would keenly listen to any news related to the forces. One of my friend's sisters had joined the CRPF, and she was my inspiration. I desperately wanted to get into the forces. Moreover, since I had a sports background in school, I always felt more inclined towards these services. Unfortunately, because of my petite stature, I couldn't make it. That was a big disappointment and the end of my dreams.

By then, my eldest sister had completed her studies and got a job. Soon my other sister followed suit and got a job as well. They had to walk to the bus stop every day to board a bus to their offices. And since they were quite beautiful, they would always garner unwanted attention.

There was one particular guy who was totally smitten by Dimple. That had added to my mother's worries. Even during their college days, my elder sisters had to deal with boys always vying for their affection. But now the situation had to be controlled as my parents had been seriously contemplating Dimple's marriage and conversations with a couple of families had been initiated. I decided

I would accompany my sisters to the bus stand. Every day, like their bodyguard, I walked along with them. The guys of our locality knew I was protective towards my sisters, and they would come and help me. We became a team to ward off the bad guys. Dimple's stalker, too, had been threatened with dire consequences if he kept up his drama. Thankfully, that worked and everything proceeded smoothly thereon.

Slowly, my parents accepted the fact that even though I had been a naughty child, I was responsible. They could see that I could do things which usually weren't expected of girls! And I could do them well. After years of feeling unwanted, I could say with pride, "Ma, I may be a girl, but I'm certainly no less than a son!"

Chapter 2
Matters of the Heart

Who doesn't want love? Even the strongest people, the evil souls, the haves and the have-nots; all want love at some point of time in their lives. It is a universal yearning. I too believe love is a beautiful feeling and one should be ready to embrace it, especially if one finds his or her soulmate at any stage of life. Love does make life better. Remembering the days when the feelings of romance started brewing in my heart, I drifted to a different world altogether.

As I began watching Hindi movies, I started understanding the attraction between the opposite sexes. As I watched romantic scenes, I would blush, wondering if this happened in real life as well. Was there a Prince Charming for me? How would I feel when I would fall in love? When would my hero hold my hand? These thoughts often flooded my mind, making me turn scarlet.

After stepping into college, I started taking care of myself. I made an effort to look nice in terms of looks and appearance. I had matured and grown up to become a rather good-looking girl and was aware of the attention I received. Since I was the one who mostly went out of the house, I took up the responsibility of buying vegetables from the *haat bazaar*. Moreover, since I was very good at bargaining and selecting the freshest of vegetables, my mother happily gave me the job.

One fine day, while I was out at the market, I met a handsome guy named Manish. His strong built and charming masculine persona instantly caught my attention. His father had a property brokerage business, and he worked with his father. He resided in a different locality, but his father had his office in ours. He seemed sincere, sophisticated and a perfect guy to fall in love with. Soon I found out that he was smitten by me and that was why he had followed me in his Maruti. But he never misbehaved, and that's why I had grown a liking for him.

Months passed by, but Manish didn't say anything, though he appeared everywhere I went. I was absolutely pissed off. However, I seriously wanted Manish to say something to me, as I was equally attracted to him. Though I was usually the one taking all the initiative for any other matter, when it came to matters of the heart, I was a little old school. I wanted him to come forward and express his love for me.

When no initiative was taken by Manish for months, I finally thought of a way out. I had to take matters into my own hands. Usually in Hindi movies, the heroine is reluctant towards the advances of the hero. She slapped the hero when he followed her, and from there on, the love story started. I thought, "Let me try to see if this works."

The next time when I was walking down my street, I noticed him following me. My eyes gleamed, and I was ready for action. I hardened my face and stopped. He, too, stopped in surprise. I turned around and slapped him hard.

"Why are you following me? What's the matter?" I frowned and said in a stern voice.

He looked at me aghast; perhaps he hadn't ever imagined I would do that. He didn't reply and quietly left. I watched him walk away with a heavy heart. That is not what I had wanted. I thought he would give an explanation, but he didn't. After that, he never followed me and I never saw him again. I really regretted slapping him. Well, the lesson learnt was that filmy solutions definitely do not work in real life.

At times I would ask myself, "Do I give the vibes of a lady don? Why do the guys in my area hesitate to approach me? Are they frightened of me?"

Whatever the reason, if someone didn't have the guts to voice his feelings for me, he didn't deserve me. As simple as that! And I was well aware that all these attractions and infatuations didn't fall into my definition of love. I still had to meet my first true love.

Around this time, my elder sister got married. Her in-laws kept on insisting that we should shift from our village to a better area. Even my parents agreed that it was time to shift from Nawada to a more developed locality. They had to get their daughters married and living in a better locality would help secure better offers. My mother always made the right decisions when it came to the buying and selling of property. And this time again, she wisely sold the house and later on, the other plot that we had in Nawada, to buy two flats in Vikaspuri. She also managed to save a good amount of money. In a few months, we shifted to Vikaspuri and began life there. We had left behind the village of Nawada, though I kept visiting the place for some years. However, the inhabitants changed and our memories of the place gradually faded as well.

* * *

After my graduation from Delhi University, I completed my post-graduation in hotel management from Vikaspuri. It was a course I enjoyed and soon joined a five-star hotel in Connaught Place. Getting a job offer from a big brand wasn't easy. As a part of my course curriculum, I had to undergo training and fortunately, I got an opportunity to work as a trainee in the same hotel. I worked really hard, as the only thing I wanted was to get absorbed into the organization.

Everybody, regardless of gender, has to go through some trials and tribulations to be successful. But being a woman, and that too an ambitious one wasn't easy! If you are a woman who isn't ready to compromise on your dignity, ethics and morals, the going gets even tougher. Ask me as I experienced it first-hand. But I had promised to myself, that no matter what, I was not going to let anyone take undue advantage of me.

The Director of the F&B department, who was my father's age, developed a major crush on me. He started asking me repeatedly to meet outside the office or on Sundays. He even asked me to stay back late in the evening. He would follow me, hover around me on the premises and try to get close to me. When I rejected his advances, he started being more vocal about his nefarious intentions. Miffed, he told me that I wouldn't get absorbed as a permanent employee if I didn't agree to his demands.

I was in a difficult situation. The old creep, whom I had started hating, was making my life miserable. I wanted to grow in life and wanted to climb up the rungs of the professional ladder, but men such as this guy were hell-bent on making life difficult for young ambitious girls. At that time, I wasn't aware of anything like the

POSH (Prevention of Sexual Harassment) law. As I had just taken a few baby steps into the corporate world, I decided I had to handle this situation tactfully. I had got to know that this man's daughter also worked in the same hotel and she was more or less the same age as me.

I befriended the girl, and she became a really good buddy. We would be seen together chatting in our free time on the hotel premises or having lunch together in the canteen. In the meantime, tactfully playing with words, I had kept the director in control. I would say diplomatically, "Sir, let me first join the hotel as an employee, then we can definitely meet."

Soon he got to know that his own daughter had become a close friend of mine. He feared that I'd reveal his lustful behaviour to her, so he stopped troubling me. Moreover, my immediate boss, the head of the department, was quite happy with the dedication I had shown towards my work during the training period. He was ready to recommend me for the job. I was elated. I had patiently worked towards my goal, and in spite of the hurdles, it had paid off. The Director, of F&B, signed my offer letter, and I became an employee of the big five-star hotel.

After joining the hotel, I disclosed the director's lusty behaviour to my department head. My boss was a nice man and very protective towards the girls reporting to him.

"You don't worry at all. No one will now even think of taking undue advantage of you," he said turning fiery.

I was working hard and gaining appreciation from my bosses and colleagues. Being a vibrant and confident girl, I did receive attention from men; I won't deny this. But I just ignored everyone. I was completely focused on my career. It had just taken off and there was no place for romance in my life at that moment. After gaining a good amount of experience in that hotel, I switched over and joined another five-star hotel chain in Bikaji Cama Place in Delhi.

In my new workplace, my colleague Sneha became a good friend to me. She shared all her secrets with me and I became her confidant. She was having an affair with a guy and they were very much in love with each other. I loved the way she talked about the cosy moments she spent with her boyfriend. She would ask me if I had anyone in my life.

I would just smile and say, "No."

"I don't believe that. You are such a smart and attractive girl, I am sure you have a long list of suitors," she said.

I laughed out. "I feel guys are scared to propose to me. I seem to frighten them away."

She couldn't understand why I said so but didn't ask anything more, as she was occupied with her own love story.

Sneha and her boyfriend wanted to go to Nainital to spend some time together. She requested me to join them as she would get permission from her parents only if she was going with a girl. Her boyfriend too had asked his friend, Sanjeev, to come along. So, the four of us embarked on a short trip to Nainital.

While the two love birds literally vanished after reaching our destination. Sanjeev and I were left to sit around, talking about random things. He spoke about his ex-girlfriend with whom he had recently had a breakup. It had left him shattered. I found him calm, mature, and understanding. We got along rather well and soon developed a good bond.

After coming back to Delhi, Sanjeev and I started hanging out. He needed someone by his side to cope with the heartbreak he was going through. I really liked him and was happy to be there for him. We shared a good chemistry and then one fine day, he proposed to me. There was not a chance that I was going to say no to him. I was already in love with him.

He would pick me up and drop me to my workplace every day. We watched movies and hung out at restaurants, sweetshops, the Lodi Garden and several other places. I enjoyed his company and the special attention. Those were beautiful days. We would often sit together in a park, enjoying each other's company. And that is where he kissed me for the first time. That was the first kiss of my life and it sent electrifying sensations down my body. My first love and my first kiss will always remain unforgettable.

I came from an orthodox family and my mother had ingrained in my mind, all through my growing years, that whenever I would find a suitable boy, I had to bring him to meet her. And I was forbidden to even think of physical intimacy before marriage. During those days, a lot of emphasis was laid on the virginity of a girl. Even though Sanjeev wanted to make love and take our relationship a step further, I did not agree, as my mother's words kept ringing in my mind. Moreover, I had this fear, "What if I get pregnant?" I might sound foolish by today's standards, but that was how we were conditioned during those days.

I brought Sanjeev to meet my family, but Sanjeev never took me to meet his. I kept insisting, but he wouldn't. Rather, he said, "My elder brother is yet to be married. How can I think of my own marriage?"

I let it remain at that, though I found it a little strange. Looking back now, it was most certainly a red flag. For me, love was something that had to culminate in marriage. We could marry later, but at least he should have introduced me to his family. I had read somewhere that you know your guy is serious about you when he doesn't keep your relationship a secret and can hold your hand even in front of his family. I didn't see any such a thing happening.

I asked Sanjeev once again, "Are you really serious about me or not?" I needed to know.

And then my worst fear came true.

"Well, the truth is that I am not able to forget my ex-girlfriend. I want to go back to her. She is my love," he said looking down and breaking my heart into a zillion pieces.

I felt the ground slipping away from under my feet. I felt so weak that I thought I'd faint. But I gathered myself and tried to control my emotions. My eyes had turned teary, but I remained quiet for a while, staring at his face that barely had any emotions. He looked away as I tried to talk to him. I wanted to discuss the matter, but he refused. He was adamant that he wanted to break up with me.

I wiped my tears and said calmly, "One day you will come to me, desperate to have me back in your life."

I don't know what made me say those words so firmly, but it was spontaneous. After coming back home, I cried a lot. He was my first love. And I had never imagined that it would end like this. It had turned out to be my first heartbreak as well.

* * *

The break-up, however, made me stronger. I was full of revenge. And that translated into me becoming more successful. That was my way of revenge. I would show him what I was capable of. I started working harder. I did some short-term professional courses along with my job and also learnt a few foreign languages to better my career prospects in the industry.

By that time, both my elder sisters were married. And my parents had started thinking about my marriage. But I didn't want to get married. I was supporting my family financially. One of my brothers was doing an engineering course, and the other one was pursuing architecture. A lot of money was being spent on their education. Apart from that, the remaining two girls in the family, my younger sister and I were yet to be married.

I had always considered myself to be a son of the family. I knew a lot of money had already been spent at my sisters' weddings. That's why I had been sponsoring the major part of my brothers' education. I just couldn't think of getting married and leaving them in the lurch.

"Papa, I don't want to get married right now. After my wedding, my husband and in-laws might not allow me to support you financially," I voiced my thoughts aloud.

"You don't worry. I will manage. Every father has to get his daughters married. It's only after your marriage, we can think of Rajji's marriage. She has also grown up," he said thoughtfully.

And so began my parents' hunt for a groom for me. Those days, a girl working in a hotel wasn't considered reputable in society. People didn't think of it as a good profession for girls. They would usually say, "A girl working in a hotel must be involved in something wrong. She often comes home late at night. Who drops her home? You can't trust her character."

It was easy for people to question a girl's character. And they did it unabashedly without the knowledge of any facts. This was one reason why a few marriage proposals didn't materialize. But the sad truth is, that you cannot even question rigid societal norms, and if you dare to do so, you are branded a rebel.

While my parents' hunt for a suitable boy was on, I immersed myself in my job. My duty was at the coffee shop of the five-star hotel. A good corporate crowd came to the coffee shop, and I was managing the area well. I noticed a man who frequently came to the coffee shop, especially during lunch hours, and gazed at me. I could see a sparkle in his eyes whenever he spotted me. He tried to talk to me a couple of times, but being an employee in the hotel, I had to attend to all my guests. I got to know that his name was Rajan Srivastava and that he worked as a finance head in a big appliances firm. His work area was close to our hotel. I could clearly see that he liked me and looked for reasons to talk to me, but I didn't pay any attention.

A few days later, a well-dressed corporate man came to our coffee shop. He came straight to me and introduced himself as Dhruv Mehta, Rajan's boss. He told me he wanted to talk about something important. I was surprised.

"Yes, please tell me," I said.

"Rajan likes you a lot and wants to marry you. Please consider a marriage proposal from his side," he said in a straightforward manner. Seeing me shocked and thoughtful, he continued, "Are you seeing someone?"

"No," I replied.

"Then do you think this proposal should be taken forward?" he asked further.

After I gathered myself, I wrote my landline number on a small piece of paper and said, “This is my home number. I think it would be good if my parents were involved.”

Though I was hesitant, I ended the conversation on that note. A couple of days later, Rajan called up and talked to my parents. My mother insisted I meet and talk to him.

“Ma, I have already met him at my hotel and I am not interested in him or marriage now. You know that,” I said, annoyed.

“Veena, you have to get married. Don’t say no. You might have met him earlier, but now meet him again as your prospective groom. The boy was nice to talk to. I think it’ll be a great match,” my mother insisted.

I was only in my mid-twenties, but according to my parents, I was crossing the nubile age for marriage. That was their biggest concern, and they did all they could to pressurize me. I was doing well in my career and all they could think of was getting me married.

By this time, I had landed a managerial role in India’s most prestigious chain of hotels. It was a huge deal. This five-star hotel was in Chanakyapuri. I called Rajan to meet me at my new workplace.

As we sat face to face, he looking at me with a gentle smile while I maintained a neutral face. All through our conversation, I kept saying false and erratic things about myself, hoping that would be a turnoff. I told them I didn’t like wearing sarees (which was a white lie), that I didn’t cook and that I wasn’t even interested in it, and also that it was difficult for me to gel with new people. All I wanted to do was piss him off so that he would change his mind about marrying me. But to my great surprise, he didn’t have a problem with any of those things. He kept saying ‘fine’ to everything I told him. *What the hell?* I thought angrily. The man had perhaps sensed my lies. It was certainly difficult to shake him off.

He talked about himself, or rather tried to impress me. He said he was an MBA in finance and his company was planning to send him to the US after a year or so. During those days, an MBA guy with a plan to move abroad was in great demand by girls as well as parents. For a moment, I too started thinking that perhaps it wouldn't be such a bad idea to get married and settle abroad.

Rajan was from Prayagraj. As I had given a favourable response, my mother went to visit his home. She wanted to meet his family and have a look at their house and living standards. She wasn't satisfied with their living standards after the visit, but she felt it didn't matter, as I would live with the boy in Delhi. He was earning well to raise his standards and have a decent life. Most importantly, he liked me. It was an ideal match in every sense.

Seeing my parents worry about my marriage, and with Rajji also waiting in line, I finally decided to take the plunge and marry Rajan. After all, there was no reason to reject him. He seemed to be ideal husband material. Apart from this, there was one more reason why I didn't want to think too much. The break-up with Sanjeev at times still gave me pangs of agony; not that I missed him, but I wanted to complete my revenge. I was already working with the best name in the hotel industry and now my revenge would be complete when I would be happily married.

Rajan and I finally got engaged. The news reached Sanjeev, and he turned up out of the blue to meet me.

"I heard that you are engaged," he said with a gloomy face.

"Yes, I am," I replied, blushing. I had a big smile on my face. I was making deliberate attempts to show him that I was very happy. I wanted him to know that I had moved on. However, I was curious.

"By the way, how did you remember me all of a sudden?" I asked him.

"Veenu, please come back. I realize I made a big mistake by leaving you ... I'm sorry," he requested in a broken voice.

"But you wanted to go back to your ex, and you said you didn't love me," I was devoid of any emotions.

"I was an idiot who couldn't understand your love. I ran after a mirage, but I have learnt my lesson now. Please, Veenu, give me another chance. I promise I'll never ever break your heart. Trust me," he almost begged, with tears in his eyes.

My prophetic words on the day of our breakup had come true. Sanjeev was in front of me repenting about what he had done and pleading that I let him back in my life.

"Sanjeev, it's not possible now. I have moved on and am going to get married," I said calmly, my revengeful heart heaving an enormous sigh of relief.

"Break off your engagement; I will give you all the happiness in the world. Please Veenu," he said, holding my hand. I could see the desperation in his eyes.

I gently pulled my hand away. "You lost me a long time ago, Sanjeev," I said gravely and went back into the house.

He was my first love, the man for whom I had shed copious tears. But I chose to move on and settle for a stable marriage.

* * *

As the days grew closer to our wedding date, Rajan and I got busy, shopping and making preparations for our wedding along with my family. Unfortunately, his family didn't approve of this marriage because of our different castes. He couldn't convince them. I was a Gupta from Delhi and he a Kayasth from Prayagraj. My parents didn't have any issue with it, but his family did. Irrespective of everything, we finally got married.

I had always tamed a dream of carrying out the traditional rituals when I stepped into my husband's house as his newly wedded wife. I imagined a *kalash* filled with rice kept at the house's main door, and me pushing the kalash with my right toe, marking my auspicious entry into the house. I saw myself stepping onto an *alta-filled* copper plate and then walking into the house, leaving my footprints on the floor. The *bahu* of the house was welcomed warmly. How beautiful that would have been. Unfortunately, it remained a dream. Rajan's parents didn't even attend our wedding, forget about welcoming me into their home. I was disappointed not to have received their blessings. There was nothing I could do. Certain things in life are just not in our control. We have to go with the flow.

Chapter 3
Married Life

I was married in November in the year 1996, and just a day after our wedding we left for Kathmandu. This wasn't planned as a special honeymoon destination, but was Rajan's official trip and we decided to club it as our honeymoon.

I was still quite disappointed that none of the post-marriage rituals had taken place. I wasn't able to make something sweet for my husband's family, which is an important ritual. I couldn't even spend any time with them.

What kind of marriage is this? The thought hit me again and again. My elder sisters used to share sweet and sour stories of the initial days of their marriage, including the *saas-bahu* sagas. They talked about their new family and new home. Their experiences fascinated me, and I had always envisioned my life as a new bride. I had found their stories so interesting and had always hoped to share mine. Fortunately, I was able to visit my in-laws in Prayagraj. Contrary to my expectations, they accepted me into the family and spent some great moments with me.

Due to the immense work pressure at the hotel, with great difficulty, I was able to get ten days of leave for my honeymoon. I had already taken leaves for the wedding previously, and then while setting up our new home at Tilak Nagar, which was a rented apartment. Rajan and I chose every single thing for our home and decorated it from scratch. It was then that I had truly started looking forward to a beautiful married life with Rajan, in spite of the hiccups.

I was excited about our honeymoon, even though it was absolutely unplanned. There were a few other colleagues of Rajan who were flying with us to Kathmandu. They weren't accompanied by their wives, but since Rajan was newly married, his boss had allowed him to take his bride along with him. I could say that I was going to a beautiful foreign locale, and not the regular honeymoon destinations like Shimla, Kullu and Manali in India, where most of my friends had gone. I couldn't contain my excitement.

Rajan's organization had put us up in a five-star hotel, one of the hotel chains where I had worked earlier. I was happy to experience the same ambience. When it came to my outfits, being a Delhi girl, I was quite fashionable then and tried to keep up with the latest trends, whether it was traditional or Western wear, with my *chuda* adorning my arms. In fact, I loved flaunting my beautiful red chuda I had selectively bought from Chandni Chowk.

I was an outgoing and vibrant girl who easily mingled with everybody, irrespective of gender. I was full of life and that added more colour to my persona. And yes, I had transformed my appearance too over the years; from being a tomboy to an attractive woman with soft, luscious hair, well-manicured and pedicured hands and feet, and just the right make-up. It was important because of the industry I worked in, where everything and everyone was required to be presentable.

Because of my lively nature, Rajan's colleagues interacted with me freely. Even the staff of the hotel were quite friendly. My friends always said that I was the life of any party or social gathering. And that's true even today.

The fact that I had become popular during our stay in the hotel in Kathmandu didn't go down well with Rajan. I slowly became aware of his possessive attitude and patriarchal beliefs.

"Why are you giving them that alluring smile?"

"Why are you trying to draw men's attention?"

"Will you stop wearing those eye-grabbing outfits?"

These were just some of the weird and shocking questions he threw at me. I was shocked at how he could he even think of me in such a manner. Eye-grabbing outfits? Alluring smile? Men's attention? I was just being myself.

I spoke to everybody as I normally do. I was not the kind of woman who would even think of drawing men's attention, and that too after I was married. No way! And what was wrong with my outfit? I never wore any revealing outfits. I always wore salwar suits, jeans or trousers and a saree. Yes, I did pick up trendy outfits, say an elegant chiffon saree or a trendy pair of jeans with a nice top, but never anything that could be called revealing.

I finally understood that the problem wasn't with my smile or my outfits, or with the way I dressed, but it was the difference in the thoughts and attitude between two people. Our perspectives were different. Was it always going to be like this? I wondered. I didn't have an answer.

From being an average-looking duckling in my childhood to transforming into a strong-headed, confident, extrovert and attractive woman, I had transitioned well. It was my overall persona that had attracted Rajan towards me. We had always been different. As they say, opposites attract. But for a man, being attracted towards a strong woman is one thing, and living with the same woman after she has become his wife is a different thing altogether. Unfortunately, not every man is capable of being with a strong woman. Most of the time, a man tries to change the woman; change the very reason that drew him towards her. He tries to chop off her wings as a result of his possessiveness, ego, jealousy, and so on. And that is the beginning of the end.

I still hoped that with time, the equation between us would change. However, Rajan and I remained rather distant because of our differing views throughout the trip. I was attached to him, but could never love him completely because of this. The free bird in me felt like a controlled woman, who was seen just like a money-making machine.

* * *

We were soon back to our routine life in Delhi. Every morning, I would quickly make breakfast as both of us had to leave for work by 7:30 in the morning. He helped me in the kitchen in whatever way he could and I admired him for that. He was very supporting that way – washed his own clothes, kneaded dough as he knew I hated doing that. We would grab some sandwiches and leave together. His office was quite far away in Faridabad. So, he would drop me first and then go to Faridabad. I won't deny that Rajan was a caring husband, but only till the time I did things the way he wanted. We would have been a perfect match if I were a submissive housewife, doing his bidding.

However, differences in our opinions led to arguments and sometimes, heated ones. They had become a part of my life. But I brushed them aside as a part of married life. I would try to leave our differences behind and try to revive the romance between us. I think that is important to keep the marriage going. I'd try to keep our love life and our differences separate, but when it started becoming a pattern, it got really difficult to show affection to a man who fought with you.

I still tried to forget those differences when we were in bed. In a way, I was doing everything to keep up the romance going in our lives. However, I didn't want a child for the next few years. There was no rush. I wanted to first give priority to my career, reach a good position, gain financial stability and only then think of a baby.

Contrary to my preaching of not having a baby too soon, I unexpectedly conceived two months after our wedding. I wasn't mentally prepared for a kid and I discussed it with my mother. Discussing this matter with my mother really helped me. She told me having the baby could help bring me and Rajan closer. Although I wasn't too happy in my heart, I did want to give our love a fair chance.

As the days passed, I warmed up to the idea of becoming a mother. Whenever I thought about the new life growing inside me, I had a smile on my face. The thought of holding my baby in my arms excited me as well. The feeling of motherhood made me forget everything else, and I looked forward to holding my bundle of joy. I took good care of myself. I ate well, relaxed, meditated and kept all the woes and worries away from my life.

My pregnancy was smooth, and I continued going to the office till the end. My organization had organized an outing to Badkhal Lake near Faridabad. Since I didn't have any problems during my pregnancy, I decided to join my colleagues. But unfortunately, at the end of the day, my water broke, and I was immediately rushed to the hospital. Both my mother and mother-in-law, along with some other family members, rushed to be by my side. They were worried but at the same time, excited to welcome the baby.

My mother wanted me to try having a normal delivery and told the doctor to wait for the labour pains to begin. So, the doctor kept me in a room and waited. Even after waiting for several hours when there was no sign of any labour pain, the doctor finally took me to the OT for a caesarian delivery. A C-section was performed, and they took out the baby. It was a baby girl. I was in tears looking at my lovely daughter; my bundle of joy, whom I named Sana. I kissed her gently. I had stepped into motherhood, a beautiful phase in a woman's life.

Everyone was elated to see the newborn baby girl. My in-laws had never visited us in Delhi, but the birth of our child finally brought them to us, and I hoped things would improve in my married life.

When I was back home, my mother stayed with me for a few days. She had to return, as she had to take care of her own home. My mom-in-law wasn't keeping well, so she couldn't take care of me and left for Prayagraj. I was on my own barely a week after the birth. I had no choice but to take care of myself as well as the baby. After a caesarian delivery, it's not easy for a woman to manage everything on her own. But I had to since there was no other option. Thankfully, my house help came to my rescue.

We had a puja and some other ceremonies for my daughter. And immediately after that, my husband was sent on a special assignment to Bhopal. This was absolutely unexpected. I realized my life was going to be really difficult in the coming days. My three months of maternity leave were going to be over soon, and then it was going to be more hectic than ever. To top it all, Rajan took his car away with him.

I applied for an extension and thankfully got three more months of leave. Now I had to seriously decide how I was going to handle things on my own. One option was to quit my job and move to Bhopal to be with my husband, but honestly, I didn't want to quit as working in this big organization was a dream for many. Moreover, my profile was quite good. I couldn't let go of the opportunity I was getting. So, I decided I would to go Bhopal for some days and live with Rajan since I was on leave. I had to assess the situation calmly. Such decisions couldn't be taken in haste.

I, along with my daughter, went to Bhopal and stayed there till I exhausted my leaves. Those days were really nice. My daughter Sana had all my attention, and I enjoyed a happy family life. Later, after giving it a lot of thought, I decided I wouldn't quit my job. Giving up in difficult circumstances wasn't something in my nature, and moreover, Rajan was supposed to come back after a year anyway.

I returned to work, but life wasn't the same anymore. I was all alone in my apartment with my baby. Watching me handle everything on my own, my mother suggested I shift to her place along with my daughter. My mother was very supportive but I decided to shift closer to my mom's house. I also hired a house help to streamline all the work. That way, Sana would be taken good care of, and I would be saved the societal pressure and questions on living with my parents.

Slowly, life was back on track. I would take the chartered bus in the morning and evening, and when I had an odd shift, one of my colleagues would drop me home. Though it wasn't easy at all, life went on in such a manner. I used to be exhausted during those days. I think every working mother has her own share of struggles, and every working mother who is juggling between work and family deserves a salute.

Rajan came from time to time and spent a few days with us. Looking back, I feel shifting into a small rented apartment close to my mother's house was a good decision.

From morning till night, I was on my toes taking care of the baby, the house, the office and all the other things in between. I would prepare lunch for myself and the baby, pack her meal, and leave her at my mother's place. My maid would come to my mother's place to take care of the baby under my mother's supervision. Then I took a chartered bus to the office.

I would work the whole day and come home completely drained. But there was no time to rest as I had to take care of the baby since the help left in the evening. I managed the household chores, got groceries, and did all the other things. I cooked dinner and sometimes had to stay awake late in the night until my daughter slept.

Life had never been so difficult at any point. I was bone-tired and never imagined that I would have to go through such a chaotic phase with neither my husband nor his family to support me. I waited impatiently for Rajan's assignment to be over so that he could be back with us. Unfortunately, his assignment was extended, much to my dismay.

Rajan and I were living separate lives. The long-distance relationship was creating a gap that was getting only larger with time. He didn't like it at all when any colleague of mine dropped me home. I tried to make him understand that sometimes I missed the chartered bus because of a delay or even due to an odd shift.

The office cab wasn't always available. And in such a situation, was there anything wrong if a colleague dropped me home? I couldn't understand his displeasure.

I expected Rajan to be sensible, and understand that I was going through a tough time managing everything on my own. I wanted him to empathize, but my husband never understood me. At times, he would even suspect me of having an affair. And that would become the point of heated arguments between us. I was pissed at all the baseless accusations he threw at me. Had he left his car with me, or perhaps helped me to buy a car, I wouldn't have been dependent on anyone, but he just wasn't ready to see my point of view.

We fought over our issues, but at the end of the day, we would reconcile.

* * *

Amidst all the struggles and fights, my daughter had turned two and a half years old. I finally took a difficult decision. It was well thought out. I decided to quit my job and move to Bhopal to be with my husband. This had to be done for the sake of the family, I felt. We were growing apart. I wanted to stay positive and work on my marriage. Though it was my own decision, I felt it was truly unfortunate that an ambitious girl like me had to quit her job which she truly loved.

After moving to Bhopal, life was relaxed, but somewhere in my heart and mind, there was a void. The void of my dreams and my ambitions that were now buried. But there wasn't anything I could do at that point in time. I focused my attention on my daughter and put in all the effort I could to bridge the differences between Rajan and me.

This was the time when someone referred my name to a hotel in Bhopal for a consulting profile. And after learning about my professional background and experience in this industry, I was offered a job. Since there wasn't any progress on the personal front, I grabbed the offer, thinking that it would give me some solace at least. Rajan didn't have any objection, perhaps because it wasn't a full-time job and it added to our income.

This consulting profile gave me enough time to balance home, kid and work. I would drop my little girl at school and then immerse myself in my work. I took up a few other consulting projects as well. Once again, I began doing well professionally. I gained a name as well as fame, and people in the city got to know me. People admired me and many times my husband would get to hear the words, 'Veena's husband'. As if that wasn't enough for Rajan, he also started feeling insecure of all the attention coming my way. Every call I got made him suspicious, and we started the same arguments.

We carried on with life until Rajan received a transfer letter. And this time, he was transferred to Noida. I didn't have any choice but to give up my work once again and shift to Noida along with him. Sometimes I feel my life has been all about shifting homes. And this wasn't the end. There was more to come!

* * *

We rented a three-BHK apartment in Noida. I set up our home once again and was back to the life of a normal housewife. I would take care of our home, bring groceries and veggies, cook meals, and take care of our daughter. Since I didn't work nor had any friends to mingle with, fewer arguments between Rajan and me took place.

I was living the life of any other girl next door, but somewhere in my heart and mind, I felt something was missing. That zeal and the excitement I used to have a few years ago were completely gone. I had always lived life to the fullest, but now I felt tied down. I wanted to fly high but felt like a bird whose wings had been clipped. I could only blame the circumstances.

By the time we were settled in Noida, my husband was asked by his firm to relocate to Puducherry. This was frustrating. I felt we were living the life of nomads. *When will this shifting end,* I thought to myself, but had no answer. Perhaps that's how life was, unexpected and full of challenges.

The fact was that Rajan's organization was making layoffs, and he was given the option of moving to the Puducherry office. After giving it much thought, my husband decided he wouldn't uproot us again. So, we unanimously decided that he would quit his job and look for something new in NCR.

I heaved a big sigh of relief. Rajan started looking for a new job, but unfortunately, nothing good was turning up. There was no income, but the expenses remained the same. We were paying the rent for the big flat, there was a car to be maintained, household expenses and then the expenses of our school-going kid. Those were difficult times, as our savings were draining. We had to make some really serious decisions.

I suggested to Rajan that I should start looking for a job. We needed a source of income at the earliest. We discussed the matter, and he agreed. So, I started looking for a job in the hotel industry. After all, someone had to work to earn a livelihood. I applied to my last organization in Delhi as they had a policy of re-joining for their ex-employees. Moreover, I have been a good performer with an impressive track record.

I went for the interview and was confident I'd get the job, but unfortunately, I wasn't selected. I was dejected, wondering what the reason for my rejection could be. Perhaps the senior person who took my interview wasn't happy with my English-speaking skills. He was very finicky about pronunciation. I admit, being from a Hindi medium background, I might not have had perfect diction, but I could speak the language, and had never faced any problem earlier. I don't know when people will understand that English is just a language and not a measure of one's intelligence. Whatever the reason was, I just assumed that I wasn't destined to work in the same organization again.

I desperately looked for a job as we had almost exhausted all our savings. In the meantime, we decided to leave the apartment, as we couldn't afford to pay the rent anymore. My mother had bought a builder's flat in Gurgaon, and it was lying vacant. So, I requested her to allow us to move in there till our financial condition improved. And my mother obliged. During those days, Gurgaon was still developing, and seeing its growth potential, my mother had planned to get settled there in the future. As I said, she was wise with her decisions regarding property.

Finally, on the basis of my experience, I got a job in a luxury resort in Gurgaon. At that time, I had no idea that working at the place would turn out to be favourable for me. So much so that it would change the direction and profession of my life. It was just the beginning of good tidings as far as my professional life was concerned.

Rajan had been trying to get a suitable job, but he had had no luck. He finally got into the real estate brokerage business. But since it was a new start, he didn't have much work.

During the same time, I started facing health issues, though I never let that affect my work. I was the main breadwinner, and the family depended on me at this point. After a check-up, I got to know that I had a fibroid in my uterus. I had to get it operated before it created more problems for me.

Life, it seemed, was finally on track. We were both working, healthy and had a beautiful daughter. It seemed like everything was great, both professionally and personally.

Chapter 4
Entry into the Security Industry

Having spent over two decades in security and EP, today I feel content that despite umpteen odds, I pursued a profession I was passionate about, especially since it was a male-dominated profession. Today, people look forward to my self-defence and security training sessions because they trust in the brand name I have created for myself. They know she is the female bodyguard who protects men and has been doing so for years. The greatest sense of satisfaction comes when I see young women taking inspiration from my journey and enquiring about a career in the protection business. And I feel that the trials and tribulations throughout this journey have been worth it.

My transition from hospitality to the security industry has an interesting story behind it. Risk and protection were something innate in me; it so happened that God threw a golden opportunity, and I grabbed it with both hands.

I was working in the banquet department of the resort and was responsible for all the arrangements. A client of ours, who was the country head of an MNC, wanted to conduct a mass interview and asked me for help in arranging and coordinating the process. The organization was into security and EP business. They had just started their operations in India and were quite bullish about their business plans all across the country.

I had always been sincere and finicky about every single detail of the responsibility given to me. Perfection was non-negotiable when it came to my job. And this was for a prestigious client of our resort. So, I left no stone unturned to make the event a success. Mark, the country head, was quite impressed by my work.

When the day was about to end, he came to me and said, "Thank you for the fantastic job. I have a proposal for you."

I had no idea what proposal he was talking about. "What proposal, sir?" I asked.

"We have hired a few business development executives for our operations in India. Unfortunately, I haven't been able to find any suitable female candidate for the job. I understand this industry of security and protection might not be preferred by women in India, but I truly want a woman on my team."

He paused a bit and, gazing at me keenly, he continued, "I feel you have that spark in you! You can do it! I know it. Would you like to work for us?" he said with a calm demeanour.

This was really unexpected. *Me in the protection world? Really?*

Mark said I had that spark in me and he was right. 'Protection' was inherent in my nature! The word 'protection' was thrilling to my ears. Waves of excitement ran through my nerves as I instantly imagined myself doing some really powerful stuff. Power, strength, courage, and adventure! These words popped up in my mind as his proposal sunk in.

Though I understood my profile wouldn't be of protection per se, but more of handling the security guards and EP services, so what? At least I would be closely associated with it. And never know, I may even turn into a protection officer in the future; in layman's language—the bodyguard. A lot of things started cropping up in my mind.

Mark further explained that since the organization had very little manpower, I would be involved in the operations as well. That would mean me going to the field, fixing security issues, and, if required, doing the protection work as well.

I was getting goosebumps listening to Mark. I had missed out on my dream to join the police or CRPF but wasn't life giving me a chance to do something very close to my heart? That tomboy, courageous and adventurous Veenu came alive in me once again.

Seeing me lost in my thoughts, Mark asked, "Any doubts in your mind, Veena?"

"No, in fact, I am quite excited about it. Thanks a lot for the opportunity. I look forward to taking up this work profile," I replied instantly.

"Perfect, but following our protocol, I would like you to go through the interview process. I will be taking the final call only after your interview," he said like a true business professional.

On the very same day, I went through a string of interviews, and I was finally selected. I was elated and excited about the new beginning in my life. A wonderful opportunity had knocked at my door when I was least expecting it. Destiny can take unexpected but pleasant turns too!

* * *

My salary in this new role was less than what I had received in the hotel industry, but I didn't mind at all. This was something I really wanted to do. I had started feeling empowered at the mere thought of protection work. Certain things come to life at their own pace. So, the flame of hope should always be kept alive.

My husband had his own good reasons for encouraging me to take up the job. He felt this was a better profile than the odd shifts in the hotel industry. Also, the MNC tag had its own charm, which lured me as well; though for me, this particular industry and my work profile were the real turn-ons. Everything else was secondary.

After joining the new firm, I was sent to Bangkok for training. It was during the training that I got to understand the nitty-gritty of the protection business. Executive protection and close protection are just the international terms or rather fancy names for the role of a 'bodyguard'.

My husband's real estate work wasn't going as well as expected and he had enough time to be with our daughter when she came back from school. I felt our life had more or less reached some level of stability. I sincerely hoped he wouldn't have any issues with my new job.

I started giving my best to my new role. I began getting good business for my firm, which generated good incentives for me as well. We were a group of four or five people who worked as Business Development Executives, but as Mark had clarified earlier, I was involved in operations as well, which required fixing the security issues on the field. I wasn't a close protection officer as per my designated work profile, but very close to that.

I keenly observed all the finer details of the EP work. Somewhere in my subconscious mind, I had this feeling that someday I would begin a business of my own. I was an employee, but my mind worked constantly thinking of myself as a future employer.

Sometimes, when I went to the field to fix security issues, the clients would look at me sceptically. They certainly didn't expect a woman in the macho world of security and protection. They would confirm with the others if I was indeed the right person. I would just smile and get down to my job. Initially, my boss sent a male colleague along with me to the field, but when I did the work on my own with confidence, there was no looking back. My boss understood soon enough that Veena didn't need a male subordinate to accompany her and that she could handle any crisis by herself. I went on EP calls and managed very well on my own. I was enjoying and loving my work immensely.

Though I was hired as a business development professional, I loved it when sometimes clients called me the protection officer. It was so empowering! It gave me a sense of fulfilment like nothing had ever before. My boss, Mark, was quite happy with my work, and my confidence soared when I received appreciation from my clients and my boss. I felt like I had finally arrived.

* * *

Everything was going just fine until the same old issues started resurfacing in my personal life. Since we were a group of people working together, and I was the only female, any of my colleagues would drop me at home. Usually, all the houses in our society had glass windows and people could see a car dropping me in front of my building. Even though I didn't have any assigned shift at odd hours, being in the protection industry where the client's safety was a top priority and issues required urgent attention, sometimes I would get home late. My neighbours started spreading rumours – the favourite pastime of people with too much time on their hands.

Later on, due to my noteworthy performance, the company provided me with a car. Now again, this raised the eyebrows of people living in the area. I think this is human nature; envy and jealousy foster where people can't easily accept someone doing well in life. More so when it is a woman.

Since our company had limited manpower, the business team was also involved in operations in the field. If there was any issue with the security professionals, the clients would call the business team and I would be more than eager to take up the EP calls. At times I would have to go even at night to fix issues if there was any problem with the existing protection team on the field. Even though I tried to make them understand the nature of my job, the people in my colony barely understood or didn't even want to try to understand what an EP's job was. I didn't let their whispered taunts affect me. I kept to myself, taking care of my family and doing my best in my workspace. Since I love Hindi songs, I would just smile and relax, humming the famous song, "*Kuchh To Log Kahenge.*"

People would often gossip behind my back, "She is earning good money and now she's got a car from her office. She must be keeping her boss happy. That's how women succeed in the corporate world."

Someone else would say, "You think she's having an affair?"

Yet another person would come up with an imaginative thought, "Affair? I feel multiple affairs! She travels so often… I am sure she has lovers in different cities."

The baseless gossip and accusations reached my husband, and he wasn't pleased at all. As always, I pacified him, giving explanations and telling him what the truth was, but I really wondered how far we could go on like this.

My boss, Mark, visited my house for lunch or dinner once in a while. He always had words of appreciation for me when he talked to Rajan. Sometimes other colleagues visited us as well, but Mark came quite frequently. His son was close to my daughter's age and Mark would bring him along. The super idle and over-vigilant ladies in my neighbourhood, always on the lookout to make up a story, would talk about this as well.

"The man is fond of Veena. That's why he comes over so often." This is what they were saying, I was told by another neighbour.

All the gossip started raising doubts in my husband's mind. Rather than using his own brain, Rajan was easily influenced by what others were saying. One day, I heard Rajan talking to his ex-boss Dhruv from his previous organization. I heard him taking my name, and I quietly listened to their conversation. I was shocked to learn that he was discussing me, my work, my boss, and all his mistrust issues. I could easily gather that Dhruv was only infusing more doubts about me in Rajan's mind. That rogue Dhruv was no less than the neighbourhood aunties who enjoyed creating rifts in the life of a couple.

I got really pissed when people tried to tarnish my character. Mark did have a soft corner for me, maybe because I was the only woman and a top performer. I knew how hard I had been working ever since I joined the firm. I had toiled doggedly to reach my targets, got actively involved in operations and emergencies, and even got a lot of appreciation from my clients. But people wouldn't understand all this because all they loved doing was assassinating a woman's character.

I ignored all the negativity around me, but my husband couldn't. Moreover, due to my company's expansion plans across India, I had to travel to different places. This made my husband even more insecure. To top it all, it was a kind of role reversal in our married life. He usually spent a major part of his time at home with our daughter while I was travelling. The role reversal or the wife being more successful professionally wasn't easily accepted by my husband. Rajan could not come to terms with it. Even though I never let the problems of my personal life affect my profession, the grief and lines of tension clearly showed on my face and mood, which even my boss began to notice.

* * *

I had lately seen my boss do his own freelancing work as executive protection officer, and many times he had got employees of the firm, including me, involved in his work. His freelancing work revenue was never shown in the company's account. I knew this was wrong, but watching him, I realized I too could take up freelancing protection work, but yes, only after I quit the firm to start on my own. Till then, I had to pull up my socks, work harder and learn everything there was to know about EP services.

I got to know that my boss was arranging protection for a Hollywood celebrity who was to come to Mumbai. I requested my boss to allow me to join the team. This was a high-profile client, and all I wanted was to keenly observe the protection role, apart from doing the necessary coordination work. I was certainly not going to be the bodyguard, but I was going to get a hang of everything involved in this operation, as it were. My boss agreed. But at home, my husband didn't like my decision to fly to Mumbai along with my boss.

He insisted I don't go. But I knew Dhruv and some of the people in his friend circle had been poisoning his mind constantly, adding fuel to fire. I wasn't doing anything wrong. I was an ambitious woman who had a passion, a vision and some goals set in life. Just because of absurd and baseless trust issues, I couldn't give up my work, or the lessons that I was getting from some amazing assignments.

"I always had my doubts that you are involved with that man," he said, his eyes filled with hatred.

"That's rubbish, absolutely rubbish!" I retorted.

"You know what people in our society say about you? They aren't wrong, actually. The promotion, car, those incentives—why do you receive all the favours from your boss?" He was fuming.

"Listen, people find it very easy to judge a woman. After a lot of hard work, when a woman rises in her career, she is said to be having an affair with her boss. They can't accept a woman breaking the glass ceiling and gaining success. Please trust me, Rajan, I am not having any affair with him. I am only concerned with my work and our future," I tried to reason with my husband. His suspicions and my explanations were becoming a vicious circle in my life.

But he kept harping on the same string and then gave me an ultimatum, "Either leave me or your job."

I was utterly frustrated. How could he be so unreasonable? I decided that I wouldn't quit my job as I had yet to learn a lot about the EP business. I had been informed some days back that my organization would shut down its operations in India. I could see the uncertainty in my career looming ahead. My husband's earnings weren't enough to run our house and the only option I had was to start my own EP work. I had to think about Sana's future, her education and everything required for us to lead a decent life. Unfortunately, my husband just couldn't understand me or all of this.

Amidst all this, Rajan read an email sent to me by Mark. Since Mark was going through a divorce now and missed his son terribly, he found solace in seeing Sana and reliving old memories when we all spent time together. But the email also showed that maybe he had some feelings for me. I was a little taken aback at the revelation, but that made Rajan's insecurity win over him. This was the last straw on the camel's back and he unleashed his anger and frustration on me. His words pierced through me, and no amount of explanation could calm him down. That's when I knew it was time! I decided to leave the house. I packed my luggage and left for my mother's home, along with my daughter. This was a big move; in fact, a rebellious one. A woman leaving her husband, who was living with his inflated male ego, wallowing in the misunderstandings he himself had created.

I lived in my parents' house for a year. When a married daughter leaves her husband and comes to her parent's house, one can imagine how the parents feel. And to add to it, relatives and neighbours make them feel even worse. But I had decided to ignore everything, as I was completely focused on the bull's eye. My goal was to get into the protection work and make it my livelihood. My mother was my biggest pillar of support. She stood by my side, steadfastly telling me to do whatever I needed to.

* * *

I kept working till my company shut down its operations in India. By then, I was all set to start my own freelancing work. During that one year at my mother's place, there came a situation when Rajan and I came to the point of divorce. Even the divorce papers were prepared, but eventually, they were not signed.

Rajan started missing his daughter and the family life he had. He started feeling a void in his life. Even my daughter missed her father a lot. He wrote me long emails about wanting us to be together again, but I doubted if he had let go of his male ego. We met at our daughter's school functions and on a couple of other occasions. I could feel Rajan was going through an emotional low, both on the personal and the professional front.

Honestly, I too didn't want a divorce. Our daughter needed both her parents. For me, my daughter's future was more important than anything else. I took a decision. I along with my daughter finally went back to my husband, and we decided to give another fresh start to our life. The new friends I had made in the one year that I was away had helped me see life in a better light. In a bid to have family moments for our daughter, I made Rajan a part of some of my singing groups and sports groups so that we could spend quality time together. It was indeed a fresh start!

Chapter 5
The Journey Commences

"I had always imagined a bodyguard to be a robust and overpowering man dressed in a black suit and wearing black goggles. And here is a woman dressed simply in a shirt and trousers! I have seen some photos of you even dressed in a saree while on duty!"

This was the reaction of a journalist who met me after hearing a lot about a female bodyguard.

I explained to her, "Don't confuse the bouncer of a nightclub with a bodyguard. And forget about what you see in the movies. Real life isn't scripted and is very different from what is portrayed on the screen. A bodyguard or going by the more sophisticated term, 'Executive Protection Officer' (EPO) or Close Protection Officer (CPO) is a mix of multiple skills; one of them being the ability to blend with the crowd and avert any risk to the client."

So, here is how I turned into a bodyguard.

After my organization shut its operations in India, I knew it was the right time to start something on my own. I now had an in-depth idea of the security business. Some clients from the organization contacted me and asked me if I would like to give them the same security services just like organization provided to them. Back then in 2003, India didn't have many trusted names in the world of executive protection. The industry was still growing, and the clients needed someone trustworthy. Since they had already seen my work, they had full faith in my calibre. This was the chance I had meticulously planned for while still working in my previous organization, and I grabbed the opportunity with both hands. It was my sheer hard work that had been noticed. To stay updated, I kept learning techniques of self-defence and martial arts as well.

Business gurus say, 'Identifying a customer's need and turning it into an opportunity is what makes a good beginning for a startup.'

I had understood this well and moreover, I was highly passionate about the line of work.

I was all set for my foray into the protection business. The first deal that I cracked was with one of Chicago's richest real estate tycoons. He was to come to Jaipur with his wife and a few other people. This was a business cum pleasure trip for him to India and he wanted me to provide EP services for the entire delegation. It was a huge task, and I was pretty excited about it.

For my readers, I will explain the term 'EP'. In layman's language, an EPO or CPO can be called a bodyguard. All the terms mean the same, but 'bodyguard' is actually a thing of the past. Even though the terms are used interchangeably, EP is a term with wider dimensions, which includes all the work of a bodyguard. While bodyguarding is more of a reactive approach, EP is a proactive approach which involves pre-planning to mitigate any risk involved in the protection work. A well-trained and well-skilled executive protection professional would use intelligence and robust technological tools to assess sites, including all the buildings and places that are important to the principal.

A bodyguard might be trained in martial arts and other defence techniques, which a CPO is too, but the very use of these techniques, while with the client, negates the purpose of EP. The CPO very strategically and smartly provides security to his client without even letting him face the threat. So, this work is more about alacrity and presence of mind, rather than letting the need for physical actions and weapons arise. Anyway, a CPO is always well-prepared for worst-case scenarios.

My client arrived in Jaipur with his friends and relatives in his private chartered aircraft. They were around twelve people. I hired a team of six people to work with me. Right from the taxi drivers and every detail of other coordination work, I was on my toes. I knew well that if I led this assignment successfully and flawlessly, there would be no looking back for me.

Since my client knew that this was my first assignment, he had brought a CPO along with him. That CPO tagged with him while I tagged with my client's wife apart from my team continuously working along with me to guard the whole delegation. So, finally, I had turned into a bodyguard. I had never heard of any lady bodyguards in India but yes, I believed I was there to stay in the business!

Since my husband's real estate work wasn't doing well and it was my first assignment in the EP business, I requested him to assist in my work. He became a part of my team. The EP team was also required to stay with the client, so we all stayed in the luxurious property where the delegation was put up.

My client's CPO was very friendly and gave me further knowledge of the work. It was like learning while working. I soon formed a good bond with my client and his wife. They were happy with the way I had made all the security arrangements for them which had required me to interact rigorously with the local authorities. Overall, I had successfully completed my maiden assignment, and my client was quite happy with me.

He said, "Veena, I'll need your protection services next time as well when I come to India. And next time, I won't bring my bodyguard with me. You will handle it all."

This was a big compliment for me. I had bagged a loyal client. I had found a profession that suited my nature and attitude. I had worked hard and had given it my all. And the result had spoken for itself.

* * *

The real estate tycoon from Chicago, the same client, returned to India after six months. But this time to Kochi. Before coming to India, he ensured that I would be providing him with EP services. Also, as I had been told earlier, this time he didn't bring his bodyguard along with him.

I flew down to Kochi while my husband stayed at home with my daughter. I hired local EP professionals there and formed a team. Having gained experience from my first stint, I did the planning and coordination confidently. I wore a business suit all the time on duty. Like any other CPO, I too always carried a small kit along with me which consisted of small tools for self-defence and a few other things. I walked like the shadow of my client, keeping a hawk's eye all around.

The client wanted to explore every bit of Kochi. I got to do it along with him. I especially loved our stay in the houseboat on the backwaters. It was an amazing experience. The chef would catch the fish from the sea and cook it. It was as fresh as it could get. The dining table would be lavishly set with classic wine and the choicest menu.

My client asked me to join him for a drink but I politely refused saying, "I don't drink alcohol."

He was a little surprised that I neither drank nor smoked. However, later on after a few assignments, I realized social drinking at times was important in this field especially when one had international clients to deal with. A little flexibility as a social drinker was permissible.

Since I was good at my job and also friendly in nature, I was well-liked by the entire delegation. Though protection professionals are not supposed to dine and hang out with their clients, they can definitely have a good time together.

The crew members of my client's private aircraft would often come and have a chat with me. As always, I enjoyed interacting with new people. However, I noticed the pilot seemed to be attracted towards me. He would try to flirt whenever he could. He would say, "You are a pretty lady bodyguard." And sometimes he even called me hot and sexy. I would just smile without giving much attention to him.

But he had something else on his mind. It all started with jokes which I took casually and dismissed, but then he started making his intentions clear. He wanted to bed me. And since we all stayed in the same hotel, it was easy for him to approach me.

The man had travelled a lot with his boss and it seemed to him casual sex was just a normal thing, irrespective of the marital status of the women he slept with. But perhaps this was his first tryst with an Indian girl. Like any other woman he had met earlier, he expected me to readily agree to his sexual advances, to be in his good books. He was quite close to my client and my client took his feedback and recommendations seriously.

However, the strongly inculcated values in me have always given me the strength to overcome such complicated circumstances in my career. Moreover, I always keep in mind what my mentor (the CPO who had accompanied this client on the Jaipur trip) had told me, "Never ever mix business with pleasure in this field."

When the pilot wouldn't stop giving me hints, I knew I had to take the bull by the horns. I told him firmly, "Look, I don't mix business with pleasure. I just mean business and want to establish myself in the world of security. Yes, if you find any loophole in my services, do let me know. Otherwise please do not expect anything else from me."

The man was stunned by my retort. He certainly wasn't expecting this. After a while, he said with a smile, "I am sorry. I respect your thoughts, Veena." After that, he never flirted with me and was rather more respectful than ever before.

I do understand that when a woman is strong and confident, and is breaking the stereotypes, and to top it all, she is attractive, men would be tempted to get close to her. But then, a woman should never lose her dignity. She must stand up to her principles no matter what. Gaining respect in a male-dominated industry takes a long time, but losing respect takes just a matter of a few seconds!

I successfully completed this assignment as well. I was paid handsomely for my EP services. The business of protection was giving me everything I wanted—a sense of empowerment, travel, interaction with new people, and most importantly good money. Apart from that I got to stay in luxurious properties and enjoyed good food. Was there anything else one needed? And the best part was that I was absolutely enjoying my profession.

* * *

I was doing well in the EP business. My reputation spread by word of mouth and I started getting more and more clients, who wanted to avail my services. Most of my clients were foreigners who needed protection during their visits to India.

Things were looking up for us now. My relatives and acquaintances gradually became aware that I was doing something of my own and I was earning well. Since I was not doing a regular job, people got curious about what exactly I was into. I told them that I was working in the area of EP, which was a business term used internationally. People hardly understood what I meant. Then I tried to make them understand in a more desi way and told them that it was my job to protect my clients; I worked as a bodyguard.

People were always taken aback. They would think that I was joking. Some would giggle at my face while others would laugh behind my back, assuming I wasn't telling them the truth. The image of a tall, broad muscular man would immediately come into their minds when they heard the word 'bodyguard' and I was definitely a misfit. It was certainly difficult to make a common man understand that protection was more about agility, presence of mind and strategy rather than physique or gender.

* * *

My dedication towards my work was paying off. I was never short of work. In between major assignments, I kept getting small EP work. Since I had a good amount of experience in the hospitality industry, many clients wanted me to take up 'evacuation planning' in the hotels where they would put up, as evacuation planning had become a part of EP work by then. What exactly was evacuation planning?

So, whenever a VIP comes and stays in a hotel, he would want his security officer to check the hotel well for emergency exits. In case of a fire, terrorist attacks or any other emergency, the exit routes and internal maps should be well understood by the CPO, so they can plan for the safe exit of the client without any trouble.

After the 2008 terrorist attack on Mumbai's Taj Hotel, evacuation planning had come more into focus. But even before this dreaded attack took place, I had been doing this job regularly as part of the protection work. I would start my evacuation planning the moment it was decided where my client would stay on arrival in the city. I really liked it when the hotel staff would walk me through the hotel and its surroundings with respect. My clients were usually tycoons or top executives of big firms, and I being the CPO of such big shots, was treated with awe and respect! The most fulfilling part was that I had earned this by my sheer hard work.

By now I had my loyal clients who would prefer me to be their close protection officer, and do all the planning whenever needed. They would refer me to other people and that's how my business started growing. Finding EP work to be quite lucrative, my husband started assisting me regularly in my work as well. I was a happy soul seeing my labour bear fruit.

There were hiccups of course as there are in any business. Despite everything, people still found it difficult to believe that a woman could protect a man. I recall an assignment where a top executive of a multinational IT company was to come to Hyderabad. The company hired me to provide him with EP services. As a part of my work, I did all the pre-planning and coordination required before the arrival of my client in India.

When I came to meet my client after his arrival in India, I saw him talking on the phone standing by the side of the car. He saw me but kept talking. He looked a little worried, and I overheard that he was enquiring about his protection officer. I waved at him and he put his phone down.

"Any problem, sir?" I asked.

"My bodyguard hasn't arrived yet," he replied with a frown.

"I am your bodyguard, sir," I said with a smile.

The man looked at me from top to bottom. "You?" The surprise was evident on his face. It was hard for him to believe that I was going to give him EP services. He certainly hadn't expected a woman to be his protection officer.

"Yes sir, I am your protection officer. And I assure you I will leave no stone unturned to give you a happy experience throughout your stay here," I said in a calm and confident voice.

I could see him force a smile on his face. He was still sceptical about me being his protection officer. But in no less than a couple of hours, he figured that I wasn't a novice at my work. After reaching the hotel, I talked to the hotel staff, got all the formalities done, and the staff escorted him to his room. He saw how well-planned and coordinated everything was. The way the hotel staff talked to me, respected me and worked perfectly in sync with my coordination, I could see my client had started gaining trust in his female protection officer.

My background in the hotel industry had its own benefits for me. I was already acquainted with some of the staff in the five-star hotel that my client was staying in. I discussed the hotel security and evacuation plan with the staff and planned ahead. Getting ahead of my usual role, I even talked of a specific menu to be curated for my client, and the executive chef himself came to me and talked in detail about my client's preferences. Being a woman, I feel I easily got access to the kitchen to oversee things. Had I been a male CPO and that too with the typical macho physique of a bodyguard, I may not have got access to the kitchen and other areas of the hotel without a fuss.

I always believed being a female would have its own advantage in the business of protection. Firstly, it was more advantageous to not look like a typical bodyguard, and merge with the crowd. Secondly, I felt women had their own sixth sense to judge any situation and lastly, women because of their inherent quality of working right down to the finer details, go beyond their purview of work like checking the meals on the menu, the aesthetics and other details. And yes, a female's pleasing personality and a subtle smile can do wonders.

I, too, went beyond my protection profile to get all his meals curated and his table managed in the way he wanted. I got specific salads that he was fond of. I left no stone unturned to make the assignment a success. After the end of the trip, the client was extremely happy.

The same man who was sceptical about a lady bodyguard in the first meeting was now saying, "If ever you happen to come to the US, do visit our office there. It would be really nice if you interact with our security team and share your experiences and suggestions with the team."

The client even wrote words of appreciation and a testimonial for me. So, that's how I earned yet another loyal client.

* * *

Many people are quite curious about what I wear when I am on duty. Usually, people are used to bodyguards in white shirts with black coats and trousers. That's how they picture a bodyguard to look like. I, however, prefer wearing coloured shirts with a black coat and trousers. My mentor had advised me that it was favourable to not look like a bodyguard because that's how you would be best placed to protect your client. He had also told me that many times he wouldn't be in formals at all, and would go to the extent of wearing sneakers because that would give him the comfort to run easily if the need arose.

When I am the only one providing protection to my client, I wear trousers. But if I have a team and I work as a Detailing Manager, I prefer wearing sarees. That's the reason why many people started calling me the 'saree-clad lady bodyguard'.

In this line of work, there were other challenges that came my way. I have been asked how I manage my work during my periods. It's the time of the month when women have to face much discomfort, especially if you have a job where you have to constantly be on the go. A CPO who is on duty can't be on leave because she is menstruating. She has to be in action, irrespective of any discomfort. I have never let menstruation become an obstacle in my work. I am always prepared. That's one reason why I prefer wearing black trousers. Also, I always carry my sanitary napkins in my bag that's kept in the car. So, even if my periods come unexpectedly, I can handle the situation. Also, I take good care of my diet and fitness regime which keeps me active even during those days.

While looking after the welfare of others and seeing that everything goes off without a hitch, I barely get time to look after myself. When I am on duty, I usually don't get time to have lunch since I am constantly guarding my clients. So, I faithfully follow the saying and have 'breakfast like a king', and that gives me the energy I need throughout the day. I keep dry fruits like cashews, apricots and other nuts handy for a quick snack. Being strong mentally as well as physically is essential in this profession.

Chapter 6
Work takes me Abroad

No matter what industry you are part of or what your job is, it always feels so good when you represent your country in a foreign land. I always made it a point to wear a saree at international EP exhibitions so that people could easily recognize it as an Indian booth. A woman EP professional from India works well to get clients into the business mode. Even though I had travelled to foreign lands during my tenure in the hospitality industry my first international trip as an EP executive floods me with nostalgia.

My freelancing work in the protection business had taken off well, and I had no dearth of work. In 2005, I started attending international exhibitions and seminars on protection. I tied up with a US-based security firm and started handling EP work for their clients travelling to India. The firm would also promote me as their independent partner from India in the exhibitions.

My first international trip was to Florida. While on my way to Florida, I had mixed feelings – the joy of growing in my profession, a little hesitancy since I was travelling all alone to a country which already had good expertise in the protection business, but at the same time, I was filled with pride and a sense of empowerment. The dream I had to be a well-known name in the security and protection business was coming true, one step at a time.

I had travelled to Florida to attend an exhibition on protection. I was the Indian business representative of the US-based security firm, my business partners in the US. The card with the lanyard around my neck read – 'Independent Business Representative from India'. It was just like a trade fair held every year in India. Clad in a saree, I handled a separate security booth. All through the exhibition, I ensured my 'Indianness' was vividly visible. I was the only one wearing a saree in the entire exhibition and I must say it had its impact. People who wanted business in India were easily drawn towards my security booth. India being a huge market for MNCs, had ample business opportunities for security work as well.

I had a very successful stint representing my booth at the exhibition. I interacted with many people and got several contacts for further collaborations. My partner firm was extremely happy with the way I had dealt with customers. Now, I have become a regular visitor to such exhibitions and other training programmes that are held globally. Slowly I joined hands with a few more international security consulting firms. All these firms would pass on the EP work to me for their clients who visited India.

During one of my visits to the US, my aunt who had been living there for several years insisted I come to her place to visit her. Even my cousins called me again and again. So, this time after the exhibition was over, I finally decided to go and meet her. She greeted me well, but then as expected, she assumed I worked as an escort to rich people. Later she and my cousins saw all the stuff I had brought from the exhibition – brochures, self-defence tools and EP-related stuff that clearly showed I was into the protection business. They were surprised as they could barely imagine that a girl from their family could work in a so-called manly field like this.

I patiently explained to them how my protection business was flourishing with mostly foreign clientele to my credit. My aunt admitted that she had been wrong about me.

"We never imagined you could do such a tough thing. We always wondered what business or work was giving her such good money," my aunt confessed and I could see the admiration in her eyes for me.

"Aunt, this business has money but you need to be worth it. You need to earn it. I give my best and charge my worth," I replied with a smile.

One of my regular clients, a top executive of an IT MNC, got to know that I was there in the US. He invited me to their office to conduct a security check and talk in their US office. It was an honour for me. I, along with one of my cousins, went to their office and sat in a coffee house right in front of the main building. After some time, two men from the organization came to me, greeted me respectfully and took me towards the office. My cousin kept watching me in awe. The fact that was I getting so much respect in a foreign land was simply unbelievable for her. After some time, sitting in the coffeehouse, she saw me coming out of the office building followed by some of the staff. I carried out the security check scrutinizing all around the building and gave them some instructions as they followed me.

My cousin was stunned to see the people taking instructions from me. She saw first-hand, what my work involved. When we came back home, she narrated the whole episode to the family. They had been living in the country for a long time, but had never got the respect I, who was just a visitor, had been shown that day. But they were happy for me and proud to see how well I was doing in my profession.

My aunt said, "I am really sorry, Veena. We were so wrong about you. You are such an empowered woman. A woman protecting a man. Wow! You have seriously proven that there's nothing called a man's profession! You are an inspiration for girls. We are all so proud of you, my girl."

I was overwhelmed hearing my aunt's words. From mistakenly thinking of me being an escort, to understanding my profession, it was a great feeling for me. Finally, my relatives started to learn what my work involved. I knew that the word would spread from my aunt to others. My aunt also talked to my mother on the phone and this time, she had no taunting questions for my mother regarding my profession, rather she was all praise for me.

Criticism had never bothered or deterred me from what I was doing. Never ever had the thought of quitting or switching the industry come to my mind. I had full faith in myself and I knew what I was doing. The validation and appreciation from my colleagues and clients were all that I needed.

***

International trips were quite frequent as the business grew. I was happy and immensely proud that Veena Gupta was a trusted name in the field of security. Something that helped me a lot was how the reputation of my work was spread by word of mouth by my happy clients and other people who were associated with me in any way professionally. But growing popularity comes with its own problems. There is no dearth of people who just can't see you flourishing. And especially when you are a woman in a male bastion, you would have a lot of hawks eyeing you, ready to bring you down at the slightest chance.

I remember a particular incident when I had travelled to the USA. I had to deliver a presentation at my partner security firm. The moment I was about to start, I realized something was wrong. My website had been hacked. When I tried to open it, a message popped up on the screen in a foreign language (it wasn't English). I couldn't understand what it said. The head of my partner firm said, "Veena, I think your website has been hacked. Let's translate and check what it means."

After translating it into English, I could only read two words: Stay away.

For a while I was shocked. And then the man reassured me, "I think it is professional rivalry, nothing else."

My partner firm understood the situation and supported me. Despite that setback, thankfully I handled the situation well enough. The trip was successful, and I was all smiles as I got ready to head back home.

There's one thing I learnt. Being an ambitious woman, I would have to deal with a number of bottlenecks, expected and unexpected, on my way to success. But that didn't mean I should mellow down, not even for a moment. The world is full of evil-minded people. They hate their competitors, and when they can't beat them in healthy competition, they adopt dirty means to bring successful people down.

Whenever I would face trying situations, I'd reason with myself that God was testing me. Making me stronger and preparing me for bigger things. And of course, the world had good people too, who would stand with me, appreciate my work and extend their support. By counting my blessings, I would face each day with resilience.

Chapter 7
Setting up Seam Group

Today, as the founder and CEO of Seam Group which provides services ranging from EP, risk management, security solutions, fire and safety installation, etc., I feel proud to have added a long list of prestigious clients to my kitty. My happy clients, along with their testimonials and recommendations, have truly helped my business gain greater heights. But scaling to this height has been a roller-coaster ride, coupled with a basketful of bitter-sweet experiences.

In 2007, a year before I set up my firm, Seam Group, a VIP executive protection assignment came through my partner firm in the USA. It was a big boost to my portfolio. The occasion was the wedding ceremony of Hollywood celebrity, Liz Hurley and businessman Arun Nayar. I had to provide EP services to the prince of a European country and his family, who were their guests. The logistics and the security were my domain. The wedding was to take place in Rajasthan, but celebrations were to take place in Mumbai as well. Since the assignment was spread out in different cities, I involved my husband, too. He was more than happy to be a part of it. He took care of our client's security in Rajasthan while I handled it in Mumbai.

While the overall assignment was executed and completed well, there was an incident which could have landed us in a difficult situation had it not been handled well. Our royal guests were staying in a five-star hotel at Nariman Point in Mumbai. I had my entire team working day and night to provide protection to my client. The female guests wanted to do some sightseeing. I arranged a few cars as a part of the security for the female guests and deployed one CPO in each car on the front seat.

The convoy of cars was out on the road in the afternoon. Though my partner firm didn't ask me to deploy any extra resources, I always make sure in such high-profile assignments, I deploy a CPO in each car. The idea is to oversee everything in each car and keep control of the driver. I was in the car that was behind the car transporting the female guests. I kept an eye on everything and coordinated wherever it was required. After some time, the car carrying the client sped ahead while my car lagged behind due to traffic. But then I noticed something worrisome.

I noticed that two young men on a bike were hounding the car in which the client was travelling. They were riding their bike very erratically and dangerously and zooming very close to the car. I was informed over the walkie-talkie by the CPO sitting in the car that the driver was feeling worried that he would either hit the bike, or some other bystander due to their rash driving. He was using all his skills to keep the car on the road, but the two on the bike kept hounding him. I also realized the clients were feeling unsafe and insecure in the car. The incident of Princess Diana's car crash due to the paparazzi hounding them was fresh in everyone's mind. I realized I had to take control of the situation in a way that did not endanger anyone's life – my client, my team and also the bikers. I realized they were doing their job, but it was endangering mine. I instructed the driver to bring our car forward, honking loudly at the bike. The two men who were now focusing on the foreigners inside the car were surprised by the loud honking and they jerked away from the car. We immediately brought our car in between their bike and the other car. I now had control of the situation, but I knew it would be a few seconds before these two again endangered themselves or us.

An important part of our EP planning is called Route Planning. It means mapping out the route on which we will be travelling in advance, along with all the exits and the turns along the road. This was an era before Google Maps became popular, so we had to memorize it. I immediately visualized the road ahead. I knew there was a left turn, which would be a route back to the hotel. I immediately screamed this out to the CPO sitting in the client's car. He was gripping the handle on the door hard as the car was swerving again and again to avoid hitting the paparazzi or the other car. As we neared the turn, we kept our car stable and exactly parallel to the client's car. I was confident the paparazzi could not see the other car. The car suddenly took the left, and they moved away from the road and towards the hotel. We, however, kept our car going at the same speed for another few hundred metres. By then, the paparazzi had realized something was wrong. We braked and parked by the side of the road. They realized then that their target for clicking pictures was gone. They, however, could do nothing, so they had to drive away in frustration.

I was informed that the other car had reached the hotel safely. I knew their planned outing had not been successful, but their security was my first priority and I was happy they were unharmed. I immediately took the route back to the hotel and rushed up to their room. As soon as I reached, I apologized to them profusely. I was afraid that they'd be very angry.

However, to my surprise, my client was very understanding. They were used to being hounded by the paparazzi, and a few times in the past had even felt threatened by their actions. But never before had they seen an EPO take such an unconventional method to keep them safe. The royal guests were quite happy with my work and praised me. This was yet another memorable EP task completed well.

***

I am a constant learner and I believe learning is an ongoing process. If I stop upgrading myself with newer things, I would be out of the race. If not me, clients would find someone else; someone better. So, I constantly attended the training programmes for EP professionals in India and abroad. Apart from the partnership with a US-based firm, I also collaborated with a few more firms having global operations in the EP industry. All these firms would pass on their EP work that needed services in India.

In 2008, I finally set up my very own company. It was initially called Seam Corporate Tours, and later on named Seam Risk Solutions, which culminated into Seam Group.

This was a huge step. I had graduated from being a freelancer to the owner of a company. I was a bodyguard and an entrepreneur too. It was a feeling of absolute pride and joy to see the nameplate with my company's name engraved on it. I had worked so hard to reach this point in life. This company was my baby, and now I had to take it to greater heights. I have always been dreamy, and my dreams have always helped me to strive for more. I truly believe that dreams keep you going, without giving you any dull moments in your career.

I have always been the kind of person who is never complacent with my accomplishments. I always have the urge to set bigger goals one after another. Achieving new milestones gives me a unique high that can't be compared to anything else. I decided I would diversify into the fire and security business as well. While working in my last organization, I met some people who were into fire safety solutions. I found this work quite challenging and interesting too. Just like the EP business, even fire security hardly had women in the area. But I was tempted to explore it and started minutely researching this area and understanding the nitty-gritty of the business.

With a lot of effort, I was finally able to set up a fire-security vertical. The work usually involved setting up of fire security systems for new and old constructions. Soon, this business took off. Usually, people in the security industry are aware of professionals and companies working in this area. I had already created a good name and reputation for myself in the EP field. Moreover, being a woman had increased my popularity thanks to the frequent media coverage I received.

I started getting projects, and I worked on them dedicatedly. But every new road has its own bottlenecks. As I always say, being a woman in male-dominated bastions has its own pros and cons. Like many other women in different fields, I too faced a set of challenges. Gender bias was a common one. But then again, the good and the bad exist together. I would say there were gentlemen too who respected and admired women for their capabilities. And it's because of the good people that this world still exists.

There was an NRI businessman who was constructing a huge educational complex in Gurgaon, and he wanted the fire-security system to be set up in the building. He had invited vendors who could do it. I, too, put up my proposal and met the man. But very soon into the meeting, I got the feeling he was not serious about my proposal. He seemed to be more interested in having a good time. He asked me many questions and told me that he would contact me soon. But I never heard from him. I understood it would be tough to get the contract, as this man didn't seem interested in my proposal at all.

Six months later, surprisingly, I got a call from the same NRI businessman. He said, "Veena, I want to talk business. Can you come to my office?"

I could sense the seriousness in his voice and tone. He indeed meant business, so I went to his office. He greeted me with warmth.

"Veena, I got to know all about the work you have done for other clients. I have, in fact, done, quite a bit of research on you and can say that you are a thorough professional. I admire you for this," he said with gravity.

"Thank you," I said politely.

"I want to work with you. These are the contract papers," he said, pointing towards some legal documents which he had kept ready.

"But…"

Before I could speak out further, he said, "Look, I will tell you everything very frankly. I felt a woman would not be able to do this job and rejected your proposal. I had received proposals from nine firms including yours, but I decided to give it to a firm which was headed by a man. But I didn't find his work up to the mark or any of the other seven people good enough to work with. I waited and then found out that you are the best vendor to take up this project."

I was more than happy. I had got the job, and that's all that mattered. I signed the contract and started my work to set up the fire security system in his complex. The project was completed well on time.

When my work came to an end, the client said with a smile, "I made the right decision to give you this project. Best wishes for your future, Veena."

I was glad that I had added yet another happy client to my list. And the best part is that he is still my client.

* * *

However successful you are in your profession, however good you are at your job, if you are a woman, there will always be people who enjoy taking jibes at you, ridiculing you and trying to shake your confidence. This is the bitter truth I experienced. I usually wore sarees whenever I went to the sites where fire security systems had to be set up. Usually, these were raw sites where construction work would be going on. Many a time, my client or the people working there didn't take me seriously. Firstly, just because I was a lady, and secondly, I was dressed in a saree.

The most common reaction I got was: "Madam, why have you come here? Please send a male."

Another reaction would be, "Madam, stay away from this site. You will fall down or get hurt."

My usual reply to them would be, "Move. Just let me do my job."

Sometimes people out of respect would bring a chair for me at the site. I would simply smile, seeing a vendor being treated like a client just because I was a woman at a construction site. I understand people weren't used to seeing a woman, and more specifically, a saree-clad woman doing assessments for fire security at raw sites. It wasn't an area many women ventured into. Even today, I think there are very few women who deal with fire safety solutions.

Just like my EP business, I was used to people's strange, and sometimes demeaning behaviour towards females even in the area of fire security. In fact, I think every industry has a mix of good and bad people. There are vultures everywhere. They don't miss a single chance of targeting their prey. But businesswomen are usually bestowed with the superb skills of handling such vultures. It's part of the game.

Sometimes after some business meetings, some men would ask for my contact number. While saving my number in his phone, a client said flirtatiously, "I am saving the number as Veena Fire," he had a suggestive smile on his lips. I shook my head.

I replied calmly but sternly, "And Veena knows very well how to extinguish the fire."

His smile was gone. He realized that he was trying to play with fire and could burn his fingers, and he took a step back. Such confidence came to me only because I was good at my work. I believe women should work hard to equip themselves with knowledge and skills. That's the only way they can get empowered and confident.

Women have their own set of challenges which perhaps only they can understand well, but putting up a fight and overcoming those challenges brings a different sense of achievement. Moreover, the journey of life is never smooth especially if you step out of your comfort zone.

Chapter 8
The Painful Separation

There is a famous song *Kabhie Kisi Ko Muqammal Jahan*… You don't get everything you desire. I think that's the harsh truth of life. Though I am not the kind of person who carries emotional baggage or grudges for long or let them impact my present, still being a sensible woman, I do feel that lucky are those people who are able to walk with their partners into the twilight of their lives. As I look back, those were very difficult days I had to go through. They were mentally and emotionally exhausting… the days when I finally decided to get a divorce.

Both my EP and fire safety business were going strong. I had hired more people while my husband was also deeply involved in the EP business. Though I was happy he was involved in my EP work, I didn't want him to give up his own real estate business. I wanted him to have his own identity and his own business. His increased involvement in my work was creating clashes of thoughts, decisions and conflicting situations.

He found this business quite fancy—travelling, luxurious stays, interaction with foreigners and above all good money. He found it all very alluring and decided for himself that he could manage it better.

One day, out of the blue, he told me, "Why don't you quit all this and just relax? Be with Sana and take care of her. Leave this business to me. Moreover, whether you agree or not, protection is a man's area. You won't be able to handle the pressure. So, let me take over."

I was shocked to hear this from him. I stared at him, aghast! *He wanted me to quit a business that was my baby?* I had toiled so hard to set it up and spent sleepless nights thinking about ways to take it further and add more loyal clients. I had constantly faced criticism and character assassination from society and now when I was at the helm of it – when it was flourishing, my husband was asking me to quit. And let him gobble up the painstakingly prepared and ready-to-eat dish? No way, I could never let that happen. This EP business was mine and I would be lifeless if it was taken away from me.

"This is not possible, Rajan," I said firmly. "I have built this business from scratch and I will never quit. How can you even think of asking me to? And this is complete bullshit that a woman can't do this work. I have been doing this very successfully for almost six years now. I have come a long way and still have a long way to go!"

"I have been assisting you in your operations. You know that very well! You couldn't have done this without me," he insisted with a cruel smile.

"Rajan, you executed a task which was brought to you," I said calmly, trying to make him understand. "But it was *I* who thought of the idea, liaised rigorously, did the PR, created a loyal client base and the projects."

We kept arguing for a while but I ended the conversation as I realized it could turn acrimonious. But I made it crystal clear that I was not quitting my EP business. Never!

* * *

Being a successful woman, that too in an unconventional field, and at the same time having a kid and a household to look after, is not easy!

People start calling you a 'superwoman' as a compliment. But I truly didn't believe in it. I didn't get into that trap of being a superwoman. I had a housekeeper and other help to take care of the house and Sana in my absence. Half of the month I would be travelling and living out of a suitcase. I would feel sad leaving my daughter and going on trips, but I didn't let any guilt get a grip on me. Life is tough in any circumstances no matter what your role is. I had to work and balance my personal life.

So, whenever I left for an assignment, I would tell Sana, "Baby, Mama is going to work, and soon she will come back to you."

My daughter slowly began to understand the nature of my work. She became a much-disciplined child who would do things on her own. Whenever I came back from my trip, I ensured I gave all my time and attention to her. I would sit with her, talk to her, drop her to school and discuss her studies. Irrespective of my hectic schedule, Sana and I shared a strong bond.

Both my husband and I had a packed schedule. Though I tried to plan our travels in such a way that either one of us stayed at home, many times both of us would be travelling together for the same assignment. During these times, my mother was a pillar of support for me. She would come over to our place and stay with Sana. By that time, I had already lost both my mother-in-law and father-in-law.

I remember a difficult time when I was travelling down south on an assignment and I received a call from my mother informing me that Sana had a high fever. Rajan was travelling too. I was time and again on audio and video calls with my help and my mother who thankfully handled everything well. Sana was taken to the doctor and recovered soon. After this incident, my husband again reiterated his views that I should let him handle the EP business. And once again I refused. The conflicts between us in business dealings too kept growing. My husband's male ego wasn't letting him come to terms that I was at the helm of affairs, the signing authority, the owner and the person high in demand by the clients. I was the face and soul of the company.

I requested him to focus on his own business. If his real estate work wasn't going well, he could switch to something else. Something where he could devote his full attention. I always maintained that my husband should have his own identity.

I still didn't mind him working with me at all, but a business couldn't run with conflicts and the male ego surfacing so frequently. Seeing him adamant in his views, I even let him handle some of our clients independently. I also let him take centre stage in many of our critical meetings. Later, I even gave him the main chair in my cabin. I did all this because I wanted mental peace, without which my business would have been severely impacted.

Sometime later, the clients he was handling started asking for me to be present in meetings and lead the EP work. They were always comfortable and satisfied with my work. Some of my long-time clients clearly said, "Veena, we want you only, not any replacement."

The EP business was my baby and I couldn't see it going down. It was my passion, my life! Judging the reaction from my clients, I decided to take control back into my hands.

This didn't go well with Rajan and he told me that he would set up his own security firm. I was shocked to hear his decision. But it was his decision and I couldn't interfere or have a say. Since he had already been interviewed by the client for the next assignment, it was agreed between us that he would be in the team till the assignment was completed.

* * *

The differences between my husband and I were increasing and the cracks in my marital life were deepening. Adding fuel to the fire were our relatives, acquaintances and people in the neighbourhood, who would keep asking my husband silly questions about my work profile, my frequent travels, working at odd hours, and coming home late. And I just hated that man Dhruv, who always made the situation worse by poisoning Rajan's mind. I knew Rajan regularly met him, and when he did, he would come back home with new arguments. Sometimes I wondered if he was the same Dhruv who had once come to me with the marriage proposal on behalf of Rajan. What kind of friend was he, trying to destroy his friend's married life? People say 'marriages are made in heaven'... I would rather people complete it: 'and they are destroyed on earth!'

At this point, my daughter Sana was in her teens. She saw the frequent heated arguments happening between us. She could understand the cracks that were deepening in our relationship. One day, she finally said, "Why don't you two get separated? I think it's good for all of us."

Those words coming from Sana made me realize that the kid had really become mature at a very young age. She was right. We needed peace in life and nothing was going right between me and my husband. Was it the time to part ways? How long could we live like this? I decided I would try to reconcile things for one final time.

I talked to my husband. "Please understand, I am doing everything for our daughter, for us. I didn't have the privilege of studying in a convent or international school. I had to compromise on a lot of things because of my family's financial situation. But I want to give Sana a better education and a better lifestyle. Just like her friends, she too wants to go on international trips. I want to give her all the happiness. Please try to understand, Rajan. Let's work on our differences and resolve them."

Rajan and I couldn't reconcile our differences. I took a deep breath and told Rajan calmly, "Then I think we better get divorced. I can't take this mental torture any longer. For all our sakes, we should part ways."

I had done all I could to stay in the marriage, but destiny had other plans. Rajan too understood that separation was the only solution as we couldn't live together any more. He started his own security company. Later, he shifted to a rented accommodation, close to our house, so that we both could take care of Sana. That was the end of my married life. I wasn't destined to have a happily ever after. But I was at peace. I was out of a toxic relationship and felt liberated. As they say, every end has a new beginning, but beginnings come with their own set of challenges.

Today Rajan and I aren't husband and wife any longer, but we share a cordial relationship and are always there for our daughter whenever she needs us. We are buddies and independent professionals. He is my travel partner too. Whenever we meet, we video call Sana. She deserves to know that her mom and dad are having a good time together. People who know me often tell her that she is just like me—a strong-headed and beautiful woman.

Chapter 9
Me, my Daughter and my Business

Two things in my life that have kept me going through the ups and downs of my life are the smiling face of my daughter Sana, who is now grown up, and my business. To overcome a bad phase of one's life, one needs something or someone they are truly passionate about. Thankfully, I had that inspiration in my life. All I wanted to do was to provide Sana with a good upbringing, a good education and the comfort she needed during her growing years. And the best part was I was achieving these goals by being in a profession that I truly loved.

Life after separation was completely different. I was a single mother who was also a businesswoman. I was all on my own; looking after my daughter and at the same time juggling my hectic work schedule. And yes, I did feel emotionally weak, and it took time for me to get over it. Thankfully, I had a good support system in family members, close friends, and my neighbours, Rohit and Niharika. Though my mother was quite worried to see our marriage fall apart, she stood by me like a rock. With their support, I was able to set up my home and bounce back.

I got back to work, planning and setting goals for my business. While I travelled, my mother stayed with Sana and took care of her. Sana was a very disciplined and understanding child. From time to time, Sana also stayed with her father when I was travelling. It had turned out well for all of us. Thankfully life was back on track.

* * *

For an assignment, I along with my team flew to Hyderabad. My visits to Hyderabad were very frequent. Since the IT industry had been in a boom and Hyderabad was a hotspot, most of my eminent clients paid regular visits to Hyderabad. This client of mine was a big name in the IT industry. Some top executives had come down to India for business meetings along with some Corporate Social Responsibility (CSR) activities. They had demanded armed EP professionals specifically.

Though armed CPOs are not usual for EP assignments, with special permission from authorities, such CPOs can be deployed. I interviewed and hired three CPOs who were authorized to use arms. So, in total, there were six EP professionals in the team and I was the Lead or Detailing Manager in business terms. Since I was a frequent visitor to the city of Hyderabad on various assignments, I coordinated various events for my clients as CPO and had been covered widely in the media as the lady bodyguard. A lot of media people knew me. They knew I was back in the city for yet another assignment and since the client was also a reputed name, they were ready to cover this event as well.

The last few assignments had been led by Rajan since I had taken a back seat, but this time I was back in my original energetic form. I was working in my own style, coordinating professionals, authorities and everything else in between. I was leading the entire security of the top executives. Once again, I went beyond the work of a CPO and looked into the finer details of my client's stay like their comfort, preferences and the dishes on the menu. I always acknowledge my experience in the hospitality sector has been a big advantage for me.

My clients were absolutely amazed to see the extra effort being put in by me which went beyond the usual hours of duty. They had never seen their bodyguards go to this extent to make their stay in a foreign country so wonderful. And here, there was an Indian woman working on her toes along with her team, to provide them an unparalleled experience.

After finishing their work, my clients had to visit a school for kids with disabilities. It was supported by their firm and this was a part of their CSR activity. The school was located in a remote area with slums all around it. It was clearly a high-risk area for my foreign clients. I called up my team and formed a strategy on how we were going to provide protection to our clients at each and every step throughout the event. Everybody was quickly in action mode.

My client usually travelled in luxurious cars but knowing the area, I arranged for ordinary cars to avoid any pomp or show. I decided to wear a saree which would help me blend in and not make me look like a typical bodyguard. When we walked into the area, the people there thought I was one of the admins of the organization. No one even could guess that I was leading the team of bodyguards. And that is exactly what I wanted! That was my security plan. I could see my client silently admiring the way I gave directions to the team for all the security arrangements. The visit went off without a hitch.

Coming from a humble background, it was my desire to master various skills that seemed interesting and had the potential to help me in my profession in any way. So, over the years, if not mastered, I had at least dabbled in various skills. One of them was to understand and interact through sign language. During the visit, I could easily interact with the kids. I was the go-between the kids and my client. The kids instantly gelled with me and seemed quite happy. In a way, I had made my client's CSR activity engaging and memorable.

The client loved my work, and they made it very clear that they wanted me to take care of their security whenever they came to India. Every assignment should end on a good note; that's what I always ensured.

* * *

Life was hectic, but I was glad everything had fallen into place. Sana was doing well in her studies and I ensured whenever I was home, all my time and attention would be on Sana. We shared a fantastic mother-daughter bond. We would hang out and, and time to time travel to some nice holiday destination chosen by Sana. She was my life, my everything!

Gradually people got to know that I had separated from my husband. People around us have different mindsets. Some understand you, some don't and some just blame the woman blindly for the separation. As if it was all her fault for failing to keep her man happy. And then, there are some men who would be rude and would try to dominate and pull down a woman who doesn't have a man at her side. They assume separated women are emotionally vulnerable and try to exploit them.

To equip myself with advanced self-defence techniques, I started training under a martial arts guru in Gurgaon. At the same time, I felt I should start imparting self-defence training to people, especially girls. This would always keep me in action and in a way help in my regular EP work as well. I started holding training sessions in local parks and other areas. Slowly more and more people outside the EP world started recognizing me.

I always kept myself updated with new self-defence techniques. Later on, seeing Sana's interest in martial arts and karate, I enrolled both of us to attend classes. While I learned the advanced techniques, she started with the basics. To receive the belts, both Sana and I went to Sweden. It was a really memorable trip. While learning a martial art, we also enjoyed the beautiful locales. Learning gave us a sense of newfound confidence, and we were hungry to learn more.

In December 2012, the Nirbhaya rape case shook the entire nation. This gruesome rape and later the death jolted me completely. I am a person who has always been an advocate of self-defence and women empowerment. Seeing her lose the battle of life, I started pondering seriously about forming an NGO that would raise the issues affecting women, give them a voice, help them learn self-defence techniques and empower them. I was anyway conducting self-defence and martial arts sessions in parks off and on, but it had to be taken up seriously now. More sessions needed to be conducted in collaboration with different organizations, institutions and even on an individual level.

So, finally, I formed my NGO – WESS (Women Empowerment Safety & Security) in 2013. The registration required fourteen members. So, I brought together fourteen members who were all empowered women, well-established in their business or profession. It took me almost six months to convince and form a consensus among them. It's not easy to convince strong women on various points as they have differing opinions, but the bigger goal i.e. empowering women, was something each one of us wanted.

I, along with my team, started creating awareness about self-defence among women. Apart from conducting training sessions, I also organized women's car rallies which became the signature event for my NGO. In 2013, I had bought a new SUV. That was the time when I heard of a car rally being organized by a reputed organization. I became a part of it with my new car. Later on, I was even given an award at the event. I thoroughly enjoyed the experience and contemplated organizing my own car rally someday.

That someday came rather soon. I organized my first all-women car rally on Women's Day in 2014. All the founding members of my NGO enthusiastically participated in the rally which was supported by the local police. There was a crowd that walked along with us with banners and posters calling out women to learn self-defence and raise their voices against crime. I still organize car rallies such as these which have become a signature event for my NGO, and to which I eagerly look forward.

I continued conducting panel discussions and events on women's empowerment through my NGO. We also tied up with schools for self-defence workshops. Our events were successful since our NGO was driven by a noble cause and was not a money-making stint. I initiated 'She Talks' as a part of my NGO where I invited strong women with remarkable achievements to talk about their inspiring life journeys. We helped to spread awareness about various issues through the NGO, and it brought me much satisfaction.

Once there was an event jointly conducted by our NGO and the local administrative authority in Gurgaon where we were to

This happens when people fail to understand the demarcation of work as far as global and local operations are concerned. The top executives of a retail giant, who were my clients, had come to India. They were bullish on opening stores in India and were launching one of their flagship stores in Punjab. The client was a big name, and it was an important assignment for me. Since the work had come to me through my partner firm, I represented the global security team and as expected, the Indian security team of the retail company wasn't involved except for some documentation work.

The head of the local security team started creating problems for me, asking me for unnecessary documents and processes to follow. I understood very well why he was doing so. He was determined to make things difficult for me. There were two things that had hurt his ego. First, why did the EP work not come to him and rather go to a woman from a different firm? Secondly, he got a feeling that the management didn't find him capable enough to handle the entire EP task. He made it an issue of prestige. He started keenly following my ways of doing work and tried to extract crucial information from me regarding work. But at this critical point, I couldn't do anything, and had to bear with him and complete the assignment.

I, along with my team, picked up my client from the Delhi airport. They were four top executives of the firm. I had arranged a fleet of cars, experienced drivers and my top EPOs for them. We dropped the executives at the hotel. We had to leave for Punjab the next morning.

We reached the city soon but there were a couple of hours left for the opening of the store. The executives checked into the hotel and decided to get ready for the event. In the meantime, I coordinated with my team of EPOs who had gone in advance to the store to assess the security situation there. The store had announced huge discounts on the day of opening. My EPOs informed me that people in the area were very excited about this new store of the retail giant. People had already started gathering around the outlet. Some had even come from the neighbouring town to buy goods.

"Keep informing me about the strength of customers," I told my CPO over the phone. "Seeing the huge discounts and today being the weekend, a lot of customers are expected. So, we have to be very careful and vigilant."

"Yes madam, it is expected there will be a long queue outside the store," he informed.

"That's normal when it's such a grand opening," I said thoughtfully. However, I was a bit surprised to hear about such a huge crowd.

It was time to take the client to the venue. The executives were seated in the cars along with the CPOs. We had a convoy of one leading car, two cars which seated the executives, a follow-up car and a backup car all manned with EPOs. I was sitting in the follow-up car and coordinating with my team.

The local security head deployed two people in our cars. His purpose was to get access to each and everything I did as part of my job. He wanted to learn my techniques and processes.

I was chatting with one of his people and realized he had decided to create more problems for me. His man told me that his boss had created hype in the media about the store opening and the executives' planned visit to the store. He had highlighted the discount and mentioned the presence of top executives on the grand opening. This was definitely a security risk to my client. We had planned to inform the media, but not in the way he had done. It was unprofessional.

But I had to be prepared for any critical situation. That's what is expected from an CPO.

We were halfway when one of my CPOs at the store called me.

"Madam, it's a huge crowd here. People are getting unruly and desperate for the opening," he said and sent me a video of the venue.

It was not just one serpentine queue; people were trying to create multiple queues. I could see people arguing and pushing each other.

"The crowd needs to be controlled; I am arriving with the client in some time. Be prepared." I had expected this situation. That's why I had taken more CPOs than usual for this assignment. Moreover, seeing the attitude of the Indian security head of the firm, who was hellbent on creating trouble for me, I was very cautious.

We were close to the venue when I noticed the paparazzi crowding the road. Local media people with cameramen were flocking to the venue.

"What the hell is this? I had heard of people going crazy at the opening of stores by big brands, but this seemed unusual to me. It was all because of the unnecessary hype created in the media, especially in the local media," I thought. I got down from the car and along with a few other CPOs started clearing the road making way for the cars that had my clients. The cars pushed through the crowd and reached the store.

My team and I safely took them inside the store. The ribbon was cut, and the store was inaugurated. The executives took a tour of the store to interact with the staff and inspect the arrangements. The store wasn't open to the public as yet. It was decided that once the executives had completed the formalities and safely left the venue, the public would be allowed in.

Moments later, I was informed by my CPOs that there was chaos happening outside the store. It all started with an argument between two customers leading to a physical fight which involved more people. A media person tried to intervene, but he was beaten badly.

A few moments later, I was informed that the crowd had gone berserk. The fight that had started between two customers had turned fierce. It seemed to be a case of old rivalry which suddenly resurfaced with an argument. People from both sides joined with thick sticks and it became a grim situation. There was a stampede and taking advantage, several people flooded inside the store.

This was now a very serious situation. People started coming towards the area where the executives were standing shocked at the turn of events. I along with my CPOs quickly created a shield around the executives. It wasn't possible to take them out from the front. Since I had already visited the store in advance and studied the map, the only way out seemed to be the emergency exit.

"Prepare the emergency exit," I shouted to my team of CPOs.

Two of my CPO's rushed towards the emergency exit which was a little away from the main area. The two security personnel deployed by the local security head were in a fix and didn't have any idea of the inside map. I realized they were good for nothing. The staff members of the store who were new hires were shell-shocked at the situation. But heeding my instructions, they immediately got into action, informed the police and took up safety positions inside the store. After all, safety of the employees was equally important. Damage to the store could be managed, but not loss of life.

I could see the worry on my client's face.

"Sir, don't worry we will take you all out safely," I reassured them.

I, along with my team, led the executives towards the exit. I called the drivers to bring the cars towards the emergency exit. My drivers had also been detailed about the external map of the store. I consider drivers as equally important resources who through their experience and expertise, can turn out to be saviours in risky situations.

The exit door was opened. I saw a few people coming towards the exit door. They had somehow got to know about the emergency exit too. Those people coming towards the exit didn't give me good vibes. My team made a human wall between the people and our client. The executives were led inside the car. That very moment a man tried to come close to one of the cars. I jumped towards him and blocked his path.

All of us got into the cars and left the venue. I could see the man sitting on the ground, holding his nose. We reached the hotel safely. I got to know that the police had arrived soon after and controlled the mob. Thankfully there was no loss of life amongst the staff or the mob and the damage to the store was minimal. Everything was back to normal after a while. I was thankful that I was able to safeguard my client.

At night, sitting in my hotel room, I tried to analyze what could have led to such chaos. The fight between the people, the paparazzi or some antisocial elements? I somehow sensed some antisocial elements were involved in the ruckus. They might have had the intention to loot the store.

I remembered when I was leaving for the venue in the morning, the security head had called me and said, "Let's meet over a cup of tea after you are back from work." He seemed in a good mood then but why didn't he call up? He had been informed about everything that happened at the store that day. I kept thinking about this till I fell asleep.

The next day we left for Delhi and reached without any incident. The client made a visit to the company's office, and I met the security head there. The client was all praise for me and my team. I could see a distasteful expression on the security head's face. We didn't talk but my eyes gave him a knowing look.

Some people just don't want to agree that certain tasks need experts!

***

There was another incident that took me to Punjab again. The top executive of a multinational beer company had planned to visit India along with his two associates. They wanted to visit the brewery in Punjab and I was given the EP task. I received the schedule for their stay in India. I formed a team and visited the brewery beforehand. I also did a recce of the hotel where they planned to stay. This was all a part of my EP job.

The top boss was a tall guy, and I was a woman CP officer with a slender build. Someone from the India office had asked him if he was fine with a female CPO. He knew well about my experience in the field and was fine with me taking up the task.

I, along with my two other CPOs, accompanied the executives to the factory. They spent a few hours at the site. It was usually the norm in the company that after a successful visit, the bosses took the Indian team to the most popular place in Chandigarh. So, we all left the site and moved towards the nightclub where the party was planned.

I had already done a security check of the nightclub as protocol of my job. This was a truly happening place which was frequented by models and other celebs of the city. I was with the top boss as his CPO while my other colleagues were with the other two executives who had come with him to India. There was loud music and a good footfall inside the club. My eyes kept scanning the people present in the club. One of the executives seemed to be quite fun-loving. He was a well-dressed smart man and freely interacted with the girls in the crowd. He told his CPO to not stand with him and let him enjoy the party.

A beautiful girl who had been watching him for quite some time with a seductive smile came to him with her drink. I was watching from a distance. The executive and the girl began a conversation. The girl was standing very close to him because the music was too loud. Just then a guy came and pushed him away.

"How dare you talk to my girlfriend?" the guy shouted as his eyes nearly popped out in anger.

The executive was shocked. "She is your girlfriend?"

"Yes, and now you bear the consequences of hitting on my girl," he said fiercely as if he would gobble up the executive. He called his friends and soon four guys with gym-toned bodies came to him. The girl was quiet. Perhaps, she hadn't expected her boyfriend to come from nowhere and spot her with the executive.

Seeing the situation go out of control, I rushed towards the executive. The other CPO too noticed the situation, but I stopped him. I felt being a woman I could handle this situation better.

"Stop, stop..." I intervened as I saw all the guys coming close to my client.

"Let me explain," I said softly, standing between my client and those guys.

Seeing me talk politely, the guys cooled down a bit. "Who are you?" the girl's boyfriend asked me.

"I am a part of his protection team. He is a foreign national and a top executive of a firm. He has come to India on a business trip. Actually, this is not his fault. Your girl came to him and they talked for a while. Perhaps he found her behaviour suggestive, but that could be due to cultural differences. Let it go, brother," I said gently in Hindi mixed Punjabi. Though I am not fluent in Punjabi, I can speak it.

The guy thankfully understood my point and decided to let the matter go. A bartender who watching all this told me that the girl's boyfriend was a relative of the nightclub owner and hailed from an influential family.

My client thanked me for handling the situation. I explained he had to be a little careful and not be too friendly with unknown people. My fellow CPO asked me how I had stopped him.

To that, I replied with a subtle smile, "Sometimes just polite communication can solve big issues. Most importantly, a woman's soft voice and a gentle smile can do wonders."

The top boss of the beer company, who was sitting away with his Indian colleagues, didn't have any idea of the entire incident. I was just happy that it didn't turn into anything acrimonious. Later on, the top boss learned about it from his associate.

The next day when I dropped him at the airport, he said, "Veena,

I must say you are a good strategist too. You understand well what strategy can work where. My confidence in you is fortified."

That compliment made my day and boosted my confidence.

I usually advise my juniors that EP work is more of a mind game and intelligence. One needs to command several skills, communication being one of them.

Chapter 10
Protecting a Criminal Lawyer

Even though I have worked on a lot of interesting EP assignments, remembering some of them still infuses a thrilling wave through my nerves. The life of a bodyguard is a mix of risk, thrill and intelligence. The best part is that you are compensated well, which is worth the risk taken. Most of my clients are foreigners or NRIs, but I have also taken up security assignments for domestic clients.

It was December 2013, when a popular lifestyle magazine published a detailed article on me captioned 'The Lady Bodyguard'. It talked about how I had been creating waves in a male-dominated profession. Reading this article, a female criminal lawyer, whose cases usually involved High Net-Worth Individuals (HNIs) called me up.

I was sitting in my office and going through a few important documents when my phone rang.

"Am I speaking to Veena Gupta, the lady bodyguard?" It was a calm and grave female voice.

"Yes, this is Veena Gupta here," I replied.

"I am Ragini Aneja. I am a criminal lawyer. I got to know that you provide protection services and you are doing very well in this profession. There's a threat to my life, and I wanted to hire you as my close protection officer," she explained.

I had heard about criminal lawyers getting life threats due to the nature of their work, but I had never seen any such cases closely.

There is a perception that female lawyers usually take up civil cases; the typical societal stereotype. But here was a lady who breaking stereotypes just like me. Even though I had upcoming assignments on my hand, I was ready to put them aside or delegate them to other EP professionals.

"Okay, let me know more details about the whole assignment," I replied to the lady.

"Let's meet. I can't tell you everything over the phone."

She was right, as these matters couldn't be discussed over the phone.

"Fine, let's meet and talk."

"I will text you the address where we can meet," the lady said.

"That's fine."

The conversation ended. By the end of this call, my curiosity had piqued. Somehow, I felt I had heard this name. I typed Ragini Aneja on Google and started exploring her. I found that she was a famous name in the legal profession and had been fighting criminal cases for several years.

It was going to be a good experience providing EP services to this lady. If my client had a serious threat, her bodyguard too had a potential risk. But there lies the real challenge of protection services.

Ragini texted me her home address for our meeting. I reached well on time. She lived in a huge bungalow in a posh locality. The guard led me into the living room. She greeted me with a gentle smile. She was wearing a saree and commanded respect. She must have been in her forties, I guessed. We sat down to discuss work. I got to know from her that she was working on a murder case that involved HNIs. Basically, it all started with a property and business dispute and led to murder. The other party's men had been following her and recently, she was threatened that if she did not let go of the case, she would be killed.

"They are powerful people but I can't give up my work because of people threatening me," she said with a toughened face. "I need residential security," she added.

"Have you informed the police?" I asked curiously.

"Not yet. They have strictly told me not to approach the police or I have to face dire consequences." She paused a bit and said further, "After much thought, I decided I would hire personal security and then decide the next course of action. But I am definitely not going to back out."

I liked Ragini's determination to not give up the case she was working on.

"For how long do you need the security?" I asked.

"Till the time I win this case," came her succinct reply.

I liked her confidence. It wasn't without reason that she was a renowned criminal lawyer.

"Still, give me a rough idea so that I can accordingly plan resources and my schedule," I said, looking at her keenly.

"I think two months. I have been working closely with a witness. This witness has to be safely produced in the court before the judge. The other party doesn't know about this witness, and I have hidden him in a safe place. Another witness has already been eliminated by them. They are dangerous people, but they have forgotten that this country is run by law and not by guns," Ragini said sternly.

We discussed the matter further, as only after assessing the whole situation, I could design the right protection strategy for my client. We also discussed the financials before I left.

This was indeed going to be one of the most risky assignments I had taken up. There is a risk every time in this business. In this case, the risk was certain and the security, too, had to be strong enough to protect the client. I arranged four close protection officers for Ragini, who would be there at her bungalow round the clock. I was going to lead the team. Ragini arranged accommodation for all of us in the guest rooms of her bungalow.

I was with Ragini like her shadow, accompanying her everywhere she went. But the first thing we did was to inform the police about the threat. Ragini had already got threatening calls a couple of times. So, the police had to investigate and track the number.

While staying with Ragini, I got to know that she was single. I didn't know if she was divorced or had never married. Following the protocol of a security professional, I didn't ask anything about her personal life. But she had developed trust in me and talked about her college life when she was pursuing law. She felt happy talking about those days. I could gather that she came from a wealthy family, but she didn't say anything about where her parents were and if she had any siblings. She also shared her experiences of handling some complicated risky cases.

Ragini seemed to be quite comfortable with me. I found she was an interesting lady, a little mysterious too, at times. But I guess that is how criminal lawyers are. Well, I was just concerned about my job, i.e., securing her life.

One day, she planned to meet the witness, and we decided that she would go in disguise. So, we got a wig for Ragini and she dressed very differently that day. She wore a pair of black goggles and we stepped out from the back of her bungalow. I had arranged a taxi for her as we knew her car was always followed. This meeting was with the witness and we couldn't take any risk.

I, along with another close protection officer, accompanied her to a place which was somewhere on the outskirts. The other close protection officer was in a different car while I was with Ragini following him. Ragini had already provided details of the location. Both the cars had drivers so that the protection officers could be agile and alert to carry out any action if needed.

We reached our destination. It was a two-storey house in a residential area. I went inside along with Ragini while the other protection officer stayed outside to keep an eye around the house. Ragini talked to the witness, who was a young man. I stood a bit away while Ragini spoke to him about the case and further course of action. The man seemed to be a little scared as he got to know that Ragini had been getting death threats. He feared if those people could kill Ragini, they could kill him, too. But understanding his concern, Ragini explained to him how she had arranged tight residential security for herself and also a complaint had been registered with the police.

Many times, a witness turns hostile at the last moment, but being an expert in her field, Ragini knew how to handle the witness. From whatever I had researched about her, she had barely lost a case. And that was the fear that had made the other party give her death threats. If you can't defeat her, kill her; that's what they had thought.

While on the way back home, Ragini said, "I am all set for the next hearing. All the evidence is in place and the witness is also ready.

Those rascals can't stop me." Ragini had a hardened expression on her face.

Ragini was always very comfortable sharing her day-to-day matters, including the case details with me. She had grown quite friendly with me, but I always tried to maintain a professional relationship with her and never took the lead to ask anything that didn't concern security.

The day for the next hearing was very close. One late evening, Ragini was working on her computer when her phone rang. It was an unknown number. She picked up.

And it was the voice that had threatened her earlier. Ragini put the phone on speaker so that I, too, could listen.

"I had told you to leave this case, but still you haven't," the man said furiously.

"Who are you? Tell your boss he can't force me to do anything," Ragini retorted sternly.

We could hear a brutal laugh on the other side.

I whispered into Ragini's ears, "Tell him you are thinking about it."

She looked at me a little surprised but understood that it was the best reply to confuse him.

"You will be chopped and pieces of your body will be discarded in such a way that no one will ever get to know where you vanished," the man threatened.

Ragini kept quiet pretending to be scared of him.

"I just love chopping human bodies."

The man laughed again.

"Lot of cases will come to you. You just have to drop this one. Think wisely, lady."

After maintaining a long silence, Ragini replied meekly, "Let me think."

"That's better, but remember, I won't let you reach the court."

The man disconnected the call.

"Bastard! He is trying to pressurize me."

"Yes, but we can't take him lightly. He never accepted that he is their henchman, right?" I said thoughtfully.

"Yes, he has never accepted, nor has he revealed his identity," Ragini replied.

"We don't know who this guy is. He always calls from a different number."

"And the number is never reachable again. He must be destroying the SIM," Ragini guessed.

"We will give the number to the police. The police need to investigate it thoroughly. He could be the other party's hire or a psycho killer with some other motive. We never know. And now, since the date of the hearing is approaching, I need to tighten your security." I said as my mind turned investigative. I had to protect my client and take her safely to the court.

It was around ten at night. I had retired to the guest room. I talked to Sana on the phone and then lay down on the bed. A few minutes later, I received a call from Ragini.

"Veena, can you come to my room?" she asked.

I was a little worried. I immediately rushed to Ragini's room. I saw Ragini sitting on her bed. The moment she saw me, she came up to me.

Holding my hand, she said, "Veena, can you please sleep in my room today? I am a little worried."

I said politely, "Madam, I can't do that."

"But why? We are females," Ragini insisted.

"Sorry madam, I can't do that. Whether my client is a male or female, I need to follow some protocols. But don't worry; I and my team are there to safeguard you. You please rest. We will take care of any risk." I bade her goodnight and came out of her room.

Since we were females and Ragini seemed a little worried after that call, I could have given a thought to sleeping in her bedroom, but I had heard of suspicious relationships between bodyguards and their clients. Moreover, relationships between females too are under the scanner. So, I feel it's always better to never break the protocols.

It was the day of the hearing. We had planned everything in detail. On Ragini's insistence, I had hired armed CPOs with proper approvals from a reputed agency. I had already sent a few CPOs to get the witness safely to a pre-decided place where we were going to pick him up. We also informed the police about the hearing date and the lingering life threat.

Once again Ragini changed her get up and we decided not to use her car. I arranged for three cars with drivers. These cars looked like normal taxis. Ragini and I got into the middle car while the front and the follow-up car had my CPOs. We all stepped out again from the back door and took a different route. Two of my team members got into Ragini's car and exited from the main gate of the bungalow. This was all planned to divert the attention of those keeping an eye on us. All the CPOs, including me, were dressed casually, and none of us looked like security professionals.

We reached a place where the witness had been waiting in a different car. The CPOs put him into our car and we proceeded towards the court. Till then, there was no one following us. We were about to reach the court when one of the CPOs who had already reached the court premises informed me that some suspicious-looking men had been waiting just outside the court.

"So, they seriously intend to kill the witness and me," Ragini said, looking tense.

"Don't worry, madam, we are here to protect you. I have already done the recce of this place and will take you in safely."

We got out of the car. All my CPOs immediately created a human shield for Ragini and the witness. Suddenly, we noticed two men coming towards us with guns. They must have recognized Ragini. As they walked towards us, I quickly pushed Ragini and the witness towards the crowd. When I looked back, I saw the men had already mingled with the crowd and one of them was raising the gun. Fortunately, he wasn't able to target Ragini or the witness, as we had fully shielded them. If he fired, the bullet could hit any one of us, but before that, we had to mitigate the risk. Either we had to find a quick escape or fire at them. Before I could take the next step, the police had already arrived at the premises. I had been expecting that. Seeing the police, people started looking at them, suspecting something was wrong on the premises. The henchmen were distracted, and we took this opportunity to rush into the court.

Ragini and the witness had finally reached the courtroom safely. We got to know that the police caught hold of the two henchmen and took them into custody. I heaved a sigh of relief. I stayed with Ragini till her work was done. She successfully produced the witness and all the evidence. After the court proceedings, my team brought her back safely to the house.

It was a hectic as well as a thrilling day for me professionally, but I was content that I had judiciously protected my client. For Ragini too, it was an electrifying experience. From receiving life threats and pressure to give up the case to finally winning it, it was a high-octane case for her. Ragini expressed her gratitude to me for all the security arrangements.

"Veena, you are truly amazing. People say I am good at assessing people and they aren't wrong. The day I saw that article in the magazine and researched more about you, I knew I had to get you as my security person. When I met you, I was one hundred per cent sure I could trust you with my security," she said with a smile.

"I just did my duty, madam, and that is what I am paid for," I replied politely.

Ragini was holding a drink. She offered me one too, but I refused. I was still on duty.

Ragini sat on her lavish sofa and said, "You know Veena, I feel really amused at your husband who couldn't get along with such a beautiful and intelligent wife."

Ragini knew about my marital status. Though at times, she had wanted to know more about my personal life, I had diverted the conversation.

"Separation was our mutual decision," I gave a crisp reply.

Ragini understood I didn't want to talk about my personal life. So, she didn't say anything more.

After finishing her drink, she said, "Veena, your assignment is going to be over in a few days, but I wanted to extend the duration of our contract if you are fine."

"But this case is over. Do you still need the EP services?" I asked.

"Actually, I wanted to hire you permanently as my protection officer," she said, keenly awaiting my response.

"This is not possible, as I have to get back to my firm. If you want, I can provide you with security professionals," I suggested to her.

"No, I want you to do this job and I will pay you five lakhs per month," she looked at me for a positive response.

Five lakhs per month! Was that the effect of the drink she was having? Why does she want to shell out so much money? I thought to myself. But I loved my freedom, and more than that I had a dream to make Veena Gupta and Seam Group a big brand in the security industry. I couldn't restrict myself to just one assignment and one client.

I politely refused Ragini's offer. I told her I'd be pursuing law and did complete my law degree in 2019. At that time, after completing my assignment, I was back at my organization. Before I took up my next assignment, Sana and I went on a holiday down south. It was time for mother and daughter to enjoy the holiday moments.

Some days later, I got to know from Ragini that the police had arrested the person who was making threatening calls. Investigating his past, police found that he had killed few women who were single. Ragini, too, was single. So, was that the reason why he was targeting Ragini? But then, why was he pressurizing her to give up the case? Didn't he have any connection with the other party? These were some questions that came to my mind, but according to Ragini, investigations were still on.

I didn't dig more into it. My work was done, and I wanted to stay away from the mess.

Chapter 11
A Digression

I call myself a woman of strength, and do every bit in my capacity to foster women's empowerment through my NGO and training programmes. But let me admit, even strong women falter and commit their own fair share of mistakes. When I look back, I wonder how I could have fallen into the trap of fake love. But when you are a single woman, fighting alone in this big, bad world, trying to overcome the trauma of a broken marriage, you let your guard down. And then when a man comes into your life who is crazy about you and is madly in love with you, you just can't help but let your heart embrace that warm fuzzy feeling.

My broken marriage had left a deep scar in my heart. As a young girl, I had always dreamt of a partner who would love me, care for me, understand me and would be the one I'd grow old with. But destiny isn't designed according to one's sweet will. My heart told me – "Veena, you don't need a man in your life to make you feel happy and complete."

"Yes, that's true," my mind reciprocated.

But then again, the same heart sometimes would give me feelings of 'I want to feel loved'. There would be a smile on my lips, and then moments later, I would forcefully brush the thought aside. I would go to bed, think about the next day's do-to list, and then close my eyes.

* * *

I was frequently invited to seminars and sessions on security and self-defence. I conducted self-defence workshops for corporate and government officials. I was a media-friendly person, and the media covered me extensively. No doubt for them, the catch was always – a female bodyguard. After one such self-defence workshop, which I had successfully concluded, a man, perhaps in his mid-thirties, well-dressed in a suit and looking a perfect gentleman, walked up to me.

"Hi Veena, I am Shobhit. Major Shobhit Sharma," he said with a pleasant smile.

"Hi," I replied with a subtle smile. I had noticed this man had been keenly watching me while I was conducting the workshop.

"I have seen you at many seminars and workshops. You are doing an amazing job."

He paused for a while and kept gazing at me with a pleasant smile. He said further, "I was there at the self-defence workshop that you conducted last week at Cyber Hub. I follow your updates on social media as well. Being a woman in the world of security and protection needs some serious guts, and you are simply superb."

He talked about a few more events that I had attended and some workshops on security that I had conducted. I kept listening to him as he kept showering appreciation for me with a sparkle in his eyes.

"Thank you for the appreciation. It seems you have been following me for quite some time," I smiled gently.

"To be honest, yes. I have become your fan, actually," he said with child-like charm.

"You said, Major... do you have an army background?" I asked curiously.

"Yes, I was a major in the army but left the services due to some family reasons. Though my father has his own business which I can join, I am looking forward to making a career in security. I have been working with a firm, but it will be great if I get to work with you." He expressed his desire to work with me.

I had been looking for a resource at a senior level as my firm was growing and EP assignments were flowing in. Most of the time, I was travelling and life was utterly busy. Discerning his army background and his deep interest in security and protection, I thought he could be a good fit for the position. My mind worked fast. As always, it was work on my mind but yes, I did notice a gleam in his eyes which wasn't just because of the work he was interested in. His smile said there was more to it. To add to it, I just learnt he had been following me everywhere.

But that's fine, I thought. I am looking for a resource and he seems appropriate and more than willing to work with me. That's all that matters, my mind argued.

"Can you mail me your resume? Maybe then we can fix up a meeting at my office," I said and gave him my card, which had my email ID.

"Yes, of course. I will mail you today itself." And he threw a pleasant smile.

I smiled back and was about to leave when he said, "Veena, hope to see you again... soon."

I nodded gently and walked away.

* * *

I met Shobhit very soon after our first encounter for a professional meeting. We discussed a lot of things and finally, he joined my firm. After Shobhit started taking up the responsibilities at my firm, I felt relaxed. He started handling EP assignments, though most of the time I was present as a Detailing Manager on specific projects. When he wasn't on duty, he would come to my NGO and support the events my NGO organized. He came and supported the car rally that we held for women's empowerment as well. What I understood was that he loved being around me. Perhaps he was infatuated with me.

He was almost eight years younger than me and, most importantly, a married man with a four-year-old son. Though he had never said anything upfront, his feelings for me were evident on his face. His openly talking about his feelings was the last thing I ever wanted to hear from him. I have always strongly believed that such emotions shouldn't be mixed up with work.

My fear, however, came true. Something that I didn't want happened. An assignment came up from an MNC client in the oil and gas industry. They needed two EP professionals to provide them with security while they visited Agra, Patna, and Pune. Shobhit and I travelled with my client as EPOs, first to Agra, then to Pune, and finally to Bihar.

While we were in Agra, one day after work, my client visited the Taj Mahal and, as EP professionals, we were with them all the while. In the premises of the Taj Mahal, Shobhit came close to me and said, "It is said that the Taj Mahal is the epitome of love, and here you can feel romance even in the air."

He stared into my eyes passionately. His eyes spoke volumes of the emotions that he was going through.

I had nothing but a cold expression on my face. In fact, I was devoid of emotions. "She wasn't his only wife. I fail to understand this love," I said bluntly.

Shobhit looked at me, shocked. He certainly hadn't expected this reply from me. Within seconds, I had brutally destroyed all the romantic feelings brewing in his heart and mind. Yes, I had done it intentionally, and I hoped he understood that there could be no romantic liaison between us.

Just like many others in the industry, he too knew that I was separated and single. For me, it was fine to think about falling in love or finding a partner. But what about him? He was a married man. Why the hell was he taking a chance on me? Did he have no morals? What about his wife and child? He was ready to cheat? Yes, he was good at his work and that is what mattered to me. Nothing else.

As planned, we went to Bihar and Pune, along with our client. Everything went well. After wrapping up our assignment, we waited at the airport lounge for our flight back to Delhi. We sipped our cups of coffee quietly. I was happy. It had been a lengthy stint, but it had gone off well. This was a new client I had added to my list, the first for me from the oil and gas industry. The client was satisfied, and I knew they would look for my EP services again whenever their top executives travelled to India. I was smiling and ready to set higher goals for the firm.

"Veena, I wanted to talk to you about something."

Shobhit's words brought me back from my world of work and dreams. He was sitting on the other side of the table. A soft smile adorned his face.

"Yes Shobhit, tell me," I said, still high on the success of my work.

He paused for a while as I looked at him.

"Veena, I am in love with you."

He blurted out, his passionate voice perfectly in sync with his intense eyes.

But this was the last thing I wanted to hear from him. Seeing the shocked expression on my face, he said further, "I had wanted to confess my feelings for a long time, but somehow couldn't muster the courage to do so. I seriously love you, Veena. I really mean it."

My face turned grave. "Shobhit, you are a married man. You have a son. How could you even think of this? I think you are mistaken about me. Yes, I am separated from my husband, but that doesn't mean I am open to hookups, frivolous affairs or any sort of romantic liaison. And that too with a married man!"

"Veena, I understand you well and that's why I respect you a lot, but please let me try to explain myself," he said, almost begging.

I looked on quietly.

"It's true I am married, but my married life is nothing but a horrendous nightmare for me. I have had a pathetic time for the last few years. For the world, I am still married, yes, but my marriage has already fallen apart. There is nothing left. The only way out for me… to breathe freely and get my life back is to get a divorce. But my wife has her own terms and conditions and says she won't let me leave peacefully under any circumstances. But I will figure out something so that the legal proceedings can be started soon."

Shobhit's face turned gloomy as he talked about his married life. He revealed how his wife and her family had made his life hell. She didn't respect his father at all. Just to save his marriage, his father had now shifted to a different house with his other son. Shobhit had already lost his mother, and seeing his father being disrespected by his wife, made his heart bleed tears.

Sometimes, his wife turned violent and even hit him. He showed his neck where there was a mark made by nails. He had been holding onto his marriage just for the sake of his son, but now it was impacting his son as well. He desperately needed to get a divorce.

I truly felt bad for him. I had no inkling that he was going through all this. Behind smiling and calm faces, there doesn't necessarily lie tranquillity and happiness, I thought. I, too, always seemed calm, with a subtle smile. But yes, for me, things were different. I was happy with the way my life was going. My daughter was doing well in her studies and I, in my profession. I didn't want anything else in my life. I was content.

I looked up. I knew Shobhit was waiting for my response.

"Shobhit, honestly speaking, I don't need a man in my life. I don't have space or time for anyone or anything romantic. For me, life is just about my work and my daughter. I respect your feelings, but I am sorry."

I was crystal clear in my head about my decision, though I could clearly see the disappointment on his face.

* * *

Shobhit didn't give up hope. He kept trying to prove his love for me at every chance. He would turn up for me every time I was in need. He even went along with me to meet my mother, where he made no attempts to hide his feelings for me in front of her. He also gelled well with Sana and she seemed to like him as well. He also talked about taking legal consultation to materialize his divorce.

Slowly, I too developed feelings for him. Seeing so much love, passion, and support from him, my heart melted. After all, I was also a human with a tender heart. I accepted his love but made it clear that he needed to finalize his divorce soon. For me, our relationship made sense only when he would be separated from his wife. I didn't want to be called a home-breaker. He assured me the legal proceeding would be done soon.

A year passed, but the divorce had not materialized. He told me that his wife had made the matter complicated, and he was working with his lawyer to find a solution. On the professional front, everything was going great for me. Shobhit and I handled a lot of projects successfully. He would even accompany me to social gatherings.

Sometime later, I received a shocking revelation from a couple who lived in my society. During a conversation with them, I got to know that they knew Shobhit and his wife socially. The two couples had been friends for a long time. They informed me that Shobhit and his wife were happily married and divorce was certainly nowhere in the scene.

Digging further, I soon realized they were right. Shobhit had just been playing with my feelings, nothing else. When I confronted Shobhit, he said he loved me but didn't want to divorce his wife. So, all that drama of divorce and legal consultations was a sham!

I was seething with anger at our next meeting.

"Everything between us is over. Just stay away from me," I hissed at him.

"But Veena ..."

I was in no mood to hear any nonsense from him. "If you utter any further bullshit, everyone in your family will be informed about the other side of your character."

Shobhit understood that it wasn't going to work anymore. A few days later, he resigned and left my organization.

By this time, Sana had completed her schooling and moved to Mumbai to pursue her higher education. It was an integrated course where she had to complete a part in Mumbai and the remaining in London. I was glad that I was able to provide Sana with a good education in good institutions. I had worked hard so that she'd never feel the paucity of anything.

Even though Rajan and I had separated, we were there to support Sana. I was happy we had formed this understanding for the sake of our daughter. Be it with his physical presence or with financial support, Rajan was always there for Sana.

Sana was a mature girl and very much career-oriented. Seeing her business-woman mother, who had struggled so much to make a name in the security business, she too was determined to be an entrepreneur and set up something of her own. I was glad to see her dreaming big and setting goals for her life at such a young age. I assured her of my unwavering support and I told her lovingly, "Your mother is there with you as a strong anchor. I will always have your back."

Chapter 12
Bollywood Came Calling

I remember another interesting assignment that kept me on my toes all through. This time, my client was an upcoming actress from the Indian film industry. I was in Bangalore giving close protection to a corporate foreign client from corporate when I received a call.

The lady on the other side of the phone said, "Hi Veena, I am Garima, manager of actress Adira Menon. I called you to enquire about the personal protection services for Adira. I hope you know Adira."

I have a very bad habit. Even though I watch movies in my free time, I don't remember the names of the actors except for the big superstars whom I have been hearing about for long. Pressuring my cerebrum a little, I realized I had heard her name and, in fact, seen her last movie too, which had done well. Even though she had short screen time in the movie, she had left the viewers crazy.

"I know Adira. I have seen her last movie. She is a promising actress," I replied.

"Yes, actually, there is a stalker who has made her life hell these days. He is following her everywhere. She fears he could harm her. That's why we decided would get her personal protection till the time the police gets hold of that stalker," Garima explained.

"Has she seen the stalker?" I asked.

"Yes, once. He had come to an event where Adira was invited as a guest. He came and took her autograph. It was just a matter of a few seconds and Adira didn't remember his face as there were many people around her. Since then, he's been following her. He came to the gym following her and waited outside. When she came out, he kissed her from behind and disappeared swiftly. Adira was petrified and all she could remember was a man of average height wearing a mask. A few days later, when Adira approached her car, a little boy came to her and handed over a letter. Before Adira could ask anything, the boy ran away," Garima explained and took a pause.

"What did the letter say?" I asked curiously. I needed to know all these details for designing security for Adira if I took up the EP work.

"The letter read: 'I love you, baby. You know something, we were passionate lovers in our last birth. Due to unfortunate circumstances, we couldn't marry, but I will surely make you my wife in this birth. You remember I met you at an event and you gave me an autograph? I was the guy in the blue shirt, the first one to take your autograph. I have been following you everywhere, sweetheart. Then I kissed you outside the gym. It was such an amazing feeling. I know where you live. I will come to your apartment and we will spend the night together,'" Garima said in a stretch.

"What the hell? He seems to be a psycho." I was shocked to know the details. I had heard of some dangerous stalkers who could go to any extent because of their disturbed psyche.

"Yes, he is. Recently, Adira went to Dubai for a show. When she came back to the hotel, a staff member delivered her a courier. It had red bridal wear along with a letter. The letter read: 'I saw your performance. It was amazing. And you looked ravishing, my wife. I have sent you bridal wear. All you have to do is when you go back to India, wear it and click a pic. Take a printout and leave it at the back of the gym. And if you don't do what I say, be prepared for terrible consequences.'" Garima's voice turned tense as she narrated the situation.

"This is really horrible. Did Adira wear the outfit?" I asked.

"No. She left that gym and even changed her residence. But she is truly scared. That's the reason she wants personal security. We explored and found you're doing very well in your profession. Moreover, Adira prefers a female bodyguard."

"Adira certainly needs protection. I would be happy to provide her EP services," I replied.

I took up the assignment and travelled to Mumbai.

I met Adira at her apartment. She was an elegant and pretty young girl. She lived in a three-bedroom apartment in Mumbai. We chatted for a long time and I got to know quite a lot about her. Though I had done basic research about her before I signed up for the work, it was good to hear from her about her family, friends and lifestyle. Her parents lived in Bangalore. She shifted to Mumbai immediately after completing her schooling. She did some modelling assignments and then auditioned for a movie. She was selected for a role in the movie. Though she wasn't the lead actress, her powerful performance was noticed. The movie did decently well. She was immediately signed for the next movie which helped her make a mark. She was working on a couple of projects and at the same time sizzled on the ramp shows. Since she was a good dancer, she also did shows in India and outside. She was making good money for herself.

But she was disturbed in the last few months because of the stalker. She was living in constant fear. But one thing she did right was that she had already informed the police about the stalker.

"Adira, now I am here for you. You just concentrate on your work and leave the worries to your protection officer. The stalker will be caught very soon. I will accompany you everywhere in a casual outfit and no one will get to know that I am your close protection officer.

Adira rented a fully furnished, one-bedroom apartment for me in a building close to her. She wanted me to be available anytime she needed. Moreover, I accompanied her everywhere she went. Whenever she attended an event or a show, I would stay away from the camera and would keep a vigilant eye all around. Whenever required, I would hire local EP professionals to join me in forming a team. Adira felt safe with me, but my eyes kept looking for the stalker.

One day, Adira received a call from her parents. I could see her facial expressions changing as she talked to them. Her face turned pale, and she was in tears.

"That stalker has found the address of my parents' home in Bangalore. He has threatened them that he would pick up my brother if I don't wear the bridal outfit. He also said that he would finish off everyone if I think of marrying someone else." Adira held her head with both her hands. Droplets of tears trickled down her soft cheeks.

It was really painful to see her in such a sad state. With fame came some side effects as well.

We travelled to Bangalore, and a police complaint was registered there as well. It was decided that her brother would go to his grandmother, who lived in a small town for some time. And neither Adira nor her parents would meet him during this duration. In the meantime, the police would do their work.

We returned to Mumbai. A few days later, I accompanied Adira to a five-star hotel where she was going to endorse a newly launched product at an event. I usually stepped out with her in disguise, wearing a wig, mask and coloured glasses. I would remove all these things only after reaching the venue. That day, I did the same. While Adira was with the promoters facing the media people and other guests, I stood away at a place from where I could keep an eye on each and everyone present there. Moments later, I saw a guy come and join the other guests sitting there. I felt I had seen the guy somewhere. I thought for a while and remembered I had noticed him at the last event that Adira had attended. Something hit my mind, and I realized this was the stalker! I had seen him at earlier events too and somewhere else too... But where? My mind was working at lightning speed! Yes, outside the studio where usually Adira went to shoot parts of her current movie. Oh god! How did it not come to my mind sooner?

Blue was his favourite colour! I had spotted him in different shades of blue. He was dressed in sky blue today as well. Garima had also said that he had first met Adira in blue. That was the day he had taken her autograph. Just then, I noticed the man moving ahead. Was he moving towards Adira? I quickly became active but noticed he went and occupied a vacant seat in the second row. I breathed a sigh of relief, but without wasting a second, I stealthily clicked a few pictures of him from different angles. I quickly informed the hotel staff and security about the stalker. The hotel security came to the hall where the event was going on but to my great surprise, the stalker had already left.

Did he get to know that he had been spotted? But how? After stressing my mind a bit, I found how. The moment I found the stalker, I texted Adira to be careful as the stalker was present at the event. I saw Adira reading the text and getting tense. The stalker must have noticed this and sensed the risk. By the time I informed the hotel security; he left from the other side of the hall. He certainly was very cunning!

The other CPO, who was close to the area where Adira was, did notice the stalker, as I had texted him as well. But since the stalker exited from the other side, the CPO couldn't catch hold of him. So, the psycho in blue had escaped. Next time, he wouldn't be so lucky. Now I had his photo.

The first thing we did after the event was to give the police a photograph of the stalker. The photograph was also sent to Bangalore police.

Looking at the photographs minutely, Adira said, "I don't know why I feel like I have seen this man. I mean not at events but somewhere else; maybe some time ago."

"Is it?" I had a spark in my eyes. "Where Adira? Think..."

Adira couldn't recall. But somehow, I felt this guy knew Adira. There was some connection. It seemed I had turned a detective too, for Adira. I just smiled, thinking of the add-on role I was playing. But I had to protect Adira from the rascal at any cost, and I fervently hoped that he would be caught soon.

Adira had been invited to an event in Delhi. This time, I advised Garima to put creatives of this event on all the social media handles of Adira. Garima used to manage Adira's SM handles. We were laying out a bait and just hoped that everything would work according to our plan. I roped in four more CPOs and deliberately planned a two-day stay for Adira in Delhi.

All the CPOs were dressed casually. We spread out in different areas of the venue and kept a close watch as Adira was busy with the event. My eyes kept looking for the man in blue, but unfortunately, he didn't turn up. I was disappointed that the bait didn't work. We went back to the hotel.

I escorted Adira to her room at around 8.30 p.m. Dinner was sent to her room. I went to the dining area to have dinner along with my fellow CPOs. We ate and clicked some pictures together. After dinner, I retired to my room. I freshened up and stretched out on the bed. I picked up my phone to check the messages. One of the CPOs had forwarded me the photos we had taken. I looked at them and noticed something in one of the photos. I zoomed in and found the stalker in the background, talking to someone. Oh God, he was inside the hotel! He was wearing a navy blue shirt!

I quickly jumped out of my bed as if I had received an electric shock. I called up the reception and also informed the hotel security. I also instructed them to inform the police and alert the security at the exit doors. I changed into a T-shirt and jeans and rushed out of my room. Adira's room was on the same floor but on a different side. Just at the turn, I stopped and noticed from a distance that the man was standing close to Adira's room. My heartbeat stopped for a moment. What was he planning to do?

The moment he turned with his back facing me, I walked fast towards him. I was close to him when he sensed the risk. He was about to run, but I jumped and caught him by his wrist. Within a few moments, he was subdued. The hotel security had arrived by then.

Later, the stalker was handed over to the police. We all heaved a big sigh of relief. This marked the successful closure of the assignment. Adira was indeed the happiest person and thanked me repeatedly. A few days later, Garima informed me that the stalker was the son of the owner of a modelling agency. Adira had visited the modelling agency during her struggling days. The stalker had seen her there, but they never interacted, as his father was the person in charge. Though Adira was never associated with the agency, the guy couldn't forget her. He admitted that blue became his colour only after seeing Adira in a blue dress at his office that day. And when she became an actress, he developed an obsession with her.

My professional journey has seen several interesting and action-packed assignments, but it's difficult to put them all down in a book. Risks never bothered me because I loved mitigating them. I keep myself updated with the advanced techniques in the security industry. I always look forward to attending training programmes organized by various security associations all over the world. I believe, that the more you are updated, the better the chances of successfully completing a project.

Chapter 13
Global Operations

I am an ambitious woman and I believe I will keep dreaming till I am breathing. Age will always be just a number for me. My next goal was to expand my business beyond the boundaries of India. It was Singapore calling…

My daughter Sana was my constant support as well. Whenever I felt low, Sana was there like an anchor. It's rightly said, that when kids grow up, they become your friends. And I am blessed to have a mature and understanding daughter like Sana. Sana matured faster than others of her age and understood well the problems I faced at different stages of my life. She had seen it firsthand during her growing-up years. More than a mother and daughter, we are bosom friends. And that's the best bonding!

There was a phase in my life when I was truly feeling low thinking about my personal life and the heartbreak. This was the time I happened to meet Rajiv Mathur, an old school friend of mine. Coincidently Rajiv too was in the security industry, but we hadn't met in the last few years. Meeting him took me back to my childhood days. Even today, Rajiv is a good family friend. He was the one who inspired me to think of going global with my business. Life does bless us with good friends who come as a catalyst to lift up our sagging morale.

Rajiv and I sat in a cafe and chatted about our lives. Rajiv knew that I was divorced, but he didn't know anything about my relationship with Shobhit and the heartbreak that I had gone through. But looking at me, Rajiv could guess there was a pain that I was trying to conceal. He knew I was a strong bubbly girl, soaring high with confidence, but he didn't find me the same that day. Even though we hadn't met in the past few years, he had kept abreast of my achievements in my profession.

Reading my face, he said, "I don't see the same Veena sitting here with me. Is there something wrong?"

That's how old-time friends are! I kept quiet, not knowing what to say.

"Is everything fine at work?" he asked, trying to read my face.

I truly felt like sharing my pain. I knew he would understand. Generally, people start judging a woman without even understanding her state of mind, the emotional hiccups she could have gone through and the circumstances in her life that could have led to disastrous ends of happy beginnings.

I was lost in my thoughts when Rajiv said again, "Veena, speaking out and sharing eases the pain."

I told him all about my relationship with Shobhit. How slowly I had started dreaming of a beautiful life with him, but never had an inkling I was being fooled. This had torn apart my heart. After a bad marriage, I always believed I didn't want a man in my life, but when love came to me with all its magic, I too, as any other normal woman, wanted to embrace it.

"Rajiv, I sometimes feel like being away from this city or maybe moving out of India," I said in a melancholy voice. "But I know that's not feasible when I have my business here."

"Running away is not a solution. I know you'll overcome all your pains. You are not the kind of woman who would be bogged down by any shocks of life. You just won't stop dreaming, I am sure." Rajiv had a subtle smile on his face.

I sat quietly, listening to him.

Rajiv said further, "Why don't you think of taking your EP business beyond borders? You are well known in the industry and have a good reputation. Start providing EP services in the APAC region. To start with, you may consider setting up your operations in Singapore. And if that works, you may shift your headquarters to Singapore and even settle there if you want. I can connect you to some people there who are in the same business."

Those words from Rajiv instantly brought a spark to my eyes. Wasn't that something I wanted too? Yes, that should be my next goal – to go global! Professional highs always helped me heal my heart. I had been thinking of running away from the places that had given me heartaches and bad memories. But here I had an opportunity that could not only help me overcome my emotional hiccups but also expand my business.

I travelled to Singapore and met Surendra Sethi, the person referred by Rajiv. Surendra worked with a Singapore-based security firm. After meeting him, I realized I knew him. We had met earlier at the Rotary Club back in India. Most of the people in the industry know each other by name or have some common connection. I met other executives of the organization and discussed a possible collaboration. That's how I had planned to start my EP business there, collaborating with a local partner and sharing their workspace initially. Moreover, since I couldn't serve the clients directly, partnering with a local firm was the best possible thing.

The security firm liked my profile and my extensive experience in the EP business. We struck a deal, and I started my work in Singapore. Incidentally, my first client was an Indian. Singapore has people from all around the world and Indians have a strong presence there. The Indian client could easily connect with me and was pleased with the way I coordinated the security assignment for him.

My first stint in Singapore brought accolades from the client, and that boosted my confidence. I started making connections, as that was how I could gain prospective clients. I started researching the market deeply and realized people often travelled to Malaysia, Indonesia and other nearby countries. Protection services were required there too. Apart from this, Dubai too was on my plan. I always kept my eyes and ears open and focused on networking, as that helps immensely in security or, for that matter, in any business.

I had found a friend in Surendra in Singapore. Our Indian roots helped us bond well. We talked about Indian food, our common culture, festivals and many other random things. Surendra always had words of praise for me. He always said, "You are an inspiration for many other girls to start thinking of a career in the security industry."

I truly felt happy to hear those words from my colleague. Usually, people are either conservative in their thoughts when it comes to women or just can't appreciate another person in the same industry who is doing well.

One day, while I was busy going through some documentation work in the office, Surendra came to me and said, "Veena, we have a new assignment. He is the owner of an IT firm and needs Executive

Protection in India. You have solid experience in handling EP work for a lot of clients in the IT industry. So, I thought you could take this up."

Surendra briefed me about the assignment and I was ready to take it up. So, I was going to manage and coordinate EP protection services for Christian Strandler for the next few days.

He travelled to different countries for his work but right now, he had sought EP service for a week in India. I was elated to travel back to India because I was hating the food in Singapore. Plus, India was home. After a week, when the assignment came to an end, Christian called me to his office in Singapore.

"Veena, you have amazingly handled the EP work. I didn't see any sign of hesitation in you at any point in time. And that shows your potential." Christian was all praise for me.

"Thank you, Christian. I take every day as a new learning and look forward to taking my work to other countries as well," I said confidently.

"That should be the attitude. You grow only when you dream high." Christian encouraged me. "What is next on your mind?"

"Dubai," I replied instantly, with dreamy eyes.

"I can connect you with some prospective clients there," Christian said.

"That would be great, Christian," I almost jumped with excitement. I had been looking for some relevant connections in Dubai for quite some time and was really grateful.

I thanked Christian for his help and stayed in touch with him.

I returned to India. Sana too came down to Gurgaon to spend time with me. Even though I had been in Singapore for a short duration, and it wasn't my first international trip, for the first time in my life I missed my country so much. The streets of Delhi, the lanes of Gurgaon, rajma chawal specially cooked by my mom, and my family and friends – Oh God! I had missed all of it so much.

I truly felt that there was no place better than India. No matter how successful I am and whatever number of global offices I set up; my heart will always beat for my motherland. There was no point in thinking of settling anywhere else.

I had already visualized the roadmap of my business. There was going to be a lot of travel and I had to keep shuttling between India and Singapore. My eyes were already on Dubai and I intended to connect with clients based in Dubai as suggested by Christian. I could do business in Dubai either by partnering with security firms there or building my own network to gain clients.

With Sana doing great in studies and my business going places, life seemed to be going great.

***

I visited Dubai to understand the security market there. I found a good demand for security consulting and other business opportunities. I availed the opportunity that knocked at my door and conducted quite a few sessions, which were much appreciated by the clients there. Christian was of great help in connecting me with some influential people. Slowly I also began business consultancy there.

The pandemic years were terrible for everyone. Like most other businesses, the EP business was also badly hit. Thankfully, even during that distressing time, I kept getting some work from time to time. Also, some backlog payments came in and that kept me going. It was indeed a very difficult time, but I sailed through it. And as I say, hard work and good connections always work.

The Singapore branch had to be handed over to a local partner when the Covid protocol kicked in. Due to reduced travel, I took up fewer assignments and coordinated efficiently over calls.

I might have managed to sail through in terms of my business, but unfortunately, I lost my father to Covid-19. My mother was distraught. The head of the family was gone. That was a huge and irreplaceable loss to our family. Tears roll down my eyes every time I remember the memorable moments I had spent with my father. But no one can fight destiny. That is life.

* * *

In my entire career, one thing that I have valued the most is building good relations. Almost all the clients I have worked with have remained friends, and are in touch with me long after the assignments are over. Being a woman in the security business where there are several ill-wishers and envious people, my business gained momentum through word of mouth and, of course, through references. All thanks to the connections I made and the goodwill they had for me.

I tried to revive my global operations after the pandemic, though it was difficult. However, during this time, I realized that it was not necessary to set up offices in every country where I had clients. I could work through partner firms in that country as I had been working for several years for my clients based in the USA. So, my business model was now majorly based on catering to global clients who came to India and other Asian countries; prominently Nepal,

Bangladesh and Sri Lanka. I had tied up with local partners in these countries for any arrangements for my clients who travelled to these particular countries.

Some of my friends tried to convince me to return to Singapore and run the business from there. Their logic was that many Indian entrepreneurs were operating from Singapore very smoothly. But I was clear that India was my base, and it was always going to be so. Yes, I'd keep travelling wherever required, but the headquarters of Seam Group would be in India itself. It was here that I belonged. Though I wanted to take my business to different countries, I would stay put on my home turf. Newspapers and journals kept calling me India's first lady bodyguard, and I was happy with all the love, respect and recognition I was getting here.

Thankfully, my EP business revived immediately in India after the pandemic; though it was a little difficult to get back to my global operations in Singapore. Yes, there are challenges in all businesses, but slowly, with proper planning, they have to be overcome. I had started receiving EP assignments through my partner in the USA and other countries and we were almost back to pre-Covid days.

With all the connections I had made in Dubai, I was the preferred bodyguard for many of my clients from Dubai, who travelled to India. I remember the pleasant experience of providing security to a Russian client, an expat in Dubai, who had travelled to Varanasi. He was absolutely mesmerized by the holy city, and I ensured he had a pleasant stay there. In Dubai, usually, EP officers weren't required often, but clients travelling out of Dubai did need security. For my Dubai operations, I would travel from time to time and stay there for a few days. All through my stay, I would make connections with the industry people and try to gain more clients. This way I was able to manage just fine.

In an interesting EP assignment, I had to provide security to the prince of a European country who was to travel to India. After finishing up his work here, he planned to travel to Dubai for a meeting with a Sheikh. My job was to provide him with executive protection in India as well as in Dubai. The prince seemed to be astonished at meeting his lady bodyguard. A lady bodyguard in the West wasn't uncommon, but he hadn't expected to meet one in India. As I explained to him the security details, he complimented me, "I must say India has beauty with brains."

I smiled. I was proud of my hard work and all the sacrifices I had made to date.

I flew with him in a private charter that landed on the Sheikh's private helipad. Many other elite guests had come for a special meet at the Sheikh's mansion which was surrounded by a huge well-guarded area. The Sheikh was indeed very rich, and this was a new experience for me. The other guests were accompanied by their protection officers as well.

I had worn a saree and let my hair loose. I knew this was going to be a comparatively relaxed assignment as the prince and the other guests were invited for lunch with the Sheikh at his mansion. Despite everything, I was mentally alert and fully prepared for any situation or crisis. I was the only female EPO among all the security professionals there. The prince proudly introduced me to the Sheikh and all the other guests, "Meet Veena Gupta, my bodyguard from India."

All eyes turned towards me, and I noticed the looks of admiration for me.

When the guests were busy with the Sheikh, the EP professionals interacted with each other, trying to learn about the industry in different countries, leading to a fruitful interaction.

It was indeed a memorable assignment with the prince. I had done a good deal of networking at the Sheikh's place, and the time spent at his mansion talking to the EPs about their work, their countries, and their culture had been an enlightening experience.

Chapter 14
Miles to Go...

When I look back at my professional journey, I feel a sense of immense satisfaction. I am proud of whatever I have achieved, and indebted to God for giving me nerves of steel to deal with whatever came my way. Giving up is very easy, but accepting challenges, breaking stereotypes and achieving success against all odds is what makes one stand out. There is a restless bug in me that doesn't let me sit complacently. No amount of achievement satisfies me; rather achieving one milestone inspires me to strive for another. And this hunger for more keeps me vibrant and energetic.

Apart from the EP assignments, I was also involved in different corporate work related to security, which was equally interesting. There was a case where the top executive of a multinational IT company had been terminated. And I had been given the task of collecting his laptop, ID card and a few other essential items. The work had come to me through my partner's security firm in the USA. The work had to be done urgently while keeping it a top secret. I was going to do this as the security professional who was acting on behalf of the global head office. The local HR department was not involved in this. So, I along with my team, went to the executive's place, collected the items and handed them over to the concerned person as per the directions given to me. These were the kind of assignments that came my way as well. Over the years, I have created a trusted and efficient brand image for myself and my security firm. And it always helped me to get varied work.

There was yet another interesting case which was different from the usual EP work I do. A beer plant in Patna, Bihar, was to be closed down. I was given the responsibility of providing protection to the plant head and bringing him out of Bihar safely. This was a high-risk assignment since there was a strong possibility of the labour union creating trouble. In fact, the plant head's life could be at risk. For this assignment, I had to recruit armed EP professionals after getting due permission from the local authorities. I acted as the Detailing Manager while my team efficiently carried out the task. I would say it was a daring operation, and the client had placed their full trust in me, knowing my history of handling risky situations. I am glad I lived up to their expectations.

There was another case where my counselling and negotiation skills were put to the test. There was a garment factory in Delhi where the workers were on strike. Since I was a female who successfully ran an NGO and was involved in social services, apart from my regular executive protection business, I was approached by the client. I had to talk to the workers, counsel them and strategically negotiate with them. There was a threat to the management from the workers. So, the management had to be provided security while the negotiations were carried out. The client found me to be a perfect fit to handle the entire task.

As the disgruntled workers waited for someone to come and talk to them, I, clad in a saree, walked up to them with a smile. They had been told that a lady from an NGO would be coming to listen to their problems. I greeted them with a namaste. I talked to them and listened to their problems and demands patiently. I could notice their anger melting. My people-handling skills in the hospitality industry have always been of great help to me. And they worked here too. Being a woman might have its own set of challenges in our society, but God has made a woman a powerhouse. I truly believed in that, and in many cases, it worked to my advantage.

If I was not on an EP assignment, I would be involved in martial arts and self-defence training. I would conduct events and always be socially active through my NGO. I was regularly covered by the media. Many times, media people would call me to let them know if I planned to organize any self-defence events, as they were always on the lookout to cover such events. The icing on the cake would be the female instructor who also worked as a bodyguard.

* * *

Over the years, I have been fortunate to not only see my hard work pay off but also recognized. I have been presented with awards by several organizations. I have been generously covered by the media that has always given me good publicity. In 2017, I was elated to receive the Women in Security shield. It was like a dream come true when I was invited to give a TEDx talk. Google India recognizing me for my achievements on Women's Day in 2022 was indeed a big boost for me. I was also awarded the first runner-up in Mrs India Queen of Substance 2015 pageant. I am also frequently invited by different associations all over the world for close protection sessions. I have been privileged to be part of such sessions in the USA, UK, Italy, and Spain among others. I take these travels as opportunities to build networks which further help me in my business. I don't shy away from saying that I am always on the lookout for business opportunities. There's nothing wrong with being ambitious.

After two decades in the security business, I have come a long way. With every passing day, I feel more and more buoyant to contribute to this industry. Some people who worked under me and were trained by me, are now doing well professionally at different places. I don't have any competitive feelings, but rather I feel proud to have mentored them. And yes, I am always on a mission to empower women through my self-defence workshops.

I believe that to stay relevant and maintain the success I have earned in this competitive world, I need to keep enriching, empowering and upgrading myself. I am a constant learner and that's the reason why I enrolled myself in several short-term courses and training programmes to keep myself relevant and competitive in the security industry. I even got a law degree in the midst of my hectic work schedule. For me, learning should never stop. Recently I completed the HEPCO course from London, and aim to bring more women in this profession by training them. This can be a game-changer in the executive protection industry in India. Though I am a woman with no armed forces background, I made a name for myself in the security industry. So, all the women out there, reading my life's journey, nothing is going to stop you if you have a dream and you are ready to chase it, come what may. If I could do it, so can you.

I am thankful to my mother, who has been such an anchor in my life. Whether it was a personal or professional hiccup, my mother was always there with her unwavering support in whatever way possible. She's always been there, motivating me even when things were at their lowest. She now accompanies me to most of the events I organize through my NGO. Also, my daughter Sana, who is a young, smart and confident woman, is always there as my friend and a solid pillar of support. I am so proud that Sana is successfully running her start-up, Odyssey Curators which is a travel company and based out of Himachal. And I am proud that I have raised my daughter to be a strong and independent woman. My ex-husband and I have maintained civil terms. We always come together for the sake of our daughter. For any important day or decision in Sana's life, the two of us are there to support and cheer her. I and my ex-husband come together for vacations with Sana so that she has family time, and doesn't miss her parents. As I look at the smart woman Sana has turned into, I am filled with a sense of pride.

Life has had its own share of ups and downs, but these are litmus tests. Some people break down, give up, and succumb to challenging circumstances, but some are just too adamant to compromise with their dreams and goals in life. And I definitely belong to the latter group. And this is not the end. For me, there is still a long way to go and still many more milestones to be achieved...

Acknowledgements

There are a lot of people who need to be thanked for supporting me at different stages of my life journey. First of all, my sincere thanks to Srishti Publishers & Distributors for believing that my roller coaster life has all the elements of motivation and deserves to be brought out to the masses.

I am grateful to Google India for rewarding me as a martial arts and self-defence instructor. Thanks to the entire media because of which people started recognizing me as India's first female bodyguard.

I thank my mother and my late father who have been strong anchors to me and believed in me despite all my tomboyish eccentricities during my growing years and my daughter Sana for standing with me through my lows and highs. Thanks to my brothers and sisters for the beautiful childhood memories that we still cherish and that are now captured in this book.

Thanks to Rohit and Niharika Khetrapal, my neighbours who have been like my extended family and taken care of Sana when I was away for work.

Thanks to all my dearest friends in the security industry – Rajiv Mathur, Maj Vashiitaa Mehraa, Col Samrendra Mohan Kumar, Rekha Gairola, Jyotsna Bhalla, Rakshit Tandon, Gary Singh, Nirali Bhatia, Ritesh Bhatia, Saurabh Srivastava and Rakesh Sharma. They have been my friends, critiques and supporters.

My first EP assignment holds a special place in my career. And whenever I think of that assignment, I am reminded of Simon Wagstaff who came as an EPO with my first client. He guided and mentored me and from there, my EP career was kickstarted. Thank you, Simon.

I am grateful to my mentors in the fire and safety industry – O.P. Wahi, Ajay Pandita, Ashish Sinha, Rakesh Arora, Vikas Saxena and Inderjeet Jaitley.

I would remain grateful to my colleagues and friends from the hospitality industry who helped me gain a professional way of life. Thank you, Ritu Dhawan, Bhawna Pandey, Sanjay Sood, Samrit Pamnani, Vikas Kapoor, Vinod Bharti and Achla Chawla.

My sincere thanks to IPS Shri Alok Mittal, who has been a mentor and the guiding force for my NGO, WESS. I also thank the female police officers Kalpana Jangra and Poonam Hooda for their constant support towards the empowering initiatives taken by WESS. I extend my gratitude to Indu Saini, Bharti Patwal, Amanpreet Kaur, Roma Kakkar, Siddharth Srivastava, Nikhil, Arvind Soni, Pooja Sharma, Shewli Dey and Ashmeeta for their valuable contributions towards WESS.

I can't thank enough my martial arts mentors Yashpal Singh Kalsi, Captain Jaipreeet Joshi, Vikas Yadav, Sanjay Singh and Anuradha Kaushik. Also, thanks to Anita Shirotri for being my life coach and my dedicated office staff Ranjana Singh, Puja Bharti, Ankit and Avatar for easing the official burden.

Some friends are always there to make me smile, overcoming the lows I am going through. Thank you, Rashmi, Poonam and Sandeep, for all the fun times we have together.

My daughter Sana's friends Rohan, Anima, Kunal, Kartik, Arpan, Nikita, Ansh and Hemant who are like my kids, have been my cheerleaders. Thanks to all of them.

Thank you, God, for giving me the nerve of steel and not letting me break down!

—Veena Gupta

Writing is a solitary journey, but even that journey needs a support system.

Thank you, Ma and Papa, for inculcating in me, the love for books.

I extend my gratitude to my publisher, Arup Bose from Srishti Publishers & Distributors who has been a strong force behind the book. Right from ideating to publishing, he has been of immense help.

My sincere thanks to the editorial team at Srishti for their tremendous support. Their feedback and suggestions have helped me grow and refine as a writer.

Thanks to the bold, beautiful and woman with a never-say-die-attitude, Veena Gupta for sharing her life journey with me and collaborating to co-author this inspirational book. I have tried to faithfully pen down Veena's life and experience as she narrated them to me.

Above all, I thank Devi Saraswati for her blessings, without which this book wouldn't have been possible.

—Kamini Kusum

About Veena Gupta

Equipped with over two decades of experience in Executive Protection, Risk Management, and Security Solutions, Veena Gupta, the founder of Seam Group Services, is also an accomplished entrepreneur, author, life coach and sought-after TEDx speaker. A postgraduate in Hotel Management and a certified Martial Arts instructor, Veena has created a niche for herself in the industry and is constantly achieving new milestones with every endeavour.

Her journey, background, and life experiences have shaped her into an accomplished motivational speaker. She has touched over one lakh lives, conducted over a hundred workshops, and over a thousand counselling sessions.

About Kamini Kusum

Kamini Kusum has a PhD in Management and has worked as an HR professional in various multinational organizations like TCS, HCL etc., for several years. She is now a full-time writer.

Being in the literary world for over eight years, Kamini has penned *Dare to Shine* a non-fiction account on leading women changemakers in India, seven novels and thirty-two digital books. Her books are well-known for their strong female leads. She gives strong voices to her female characters, creating empowered heroines.

Her fiction books explore the romance genre with a mix of drama, thrill and suspense. Her works *Twisted Temptations, Difficult Girls, Gunpoint Groom, Honey & the Moon, A New Dawn* and *Queen* (Hindi) have charmed readers across the globe. Her books have been on Amazon Bestsellers lists and have been reviewed by renowned journals like *Mid-Day, Deccan Herald, The Statesman,* and *Hindustan Times* among others. She is the recipient of the Munshi Premchand Award 2024 for her work in the field of literature.

Kamini has been a part of several literary sessions and panel discussions. She has also spoken at educational institutions and literary events, where she encourages and guides budding writers.